D0468631

Sierra Nevada Wildflowers

Elizabeth L. Horn

Mountain Press Publishing Company
Missoula, Montana
1998

Third Printing, February 2006

Library of Congress Cataloging-in-Publication Data

Horn, Elizabeth L.
    Sierra Nevada wildflowers / Elizabeth L. Horn.
        p.   cm.
    Includes bibliographical references (p.   ) and index.
    ISBN 0-87842-388-5 (alk. paper)
    1. Wildflowers—Sierra Nevada (Calif. and Nev.)—Identification.
    2. Wild flowers—Sierra Nevada (Calif. and Nev.)—Pictorial works.
    I. Title.
    QK149.H638   1998   98-37890
    582. 13'09794'4—dc21   CIP

PRINTED IN HONG KONG

Mountain Press Publishing Company
P.O. Box 2399
Missoula, Montana 59806
406-728-1900

Contents

Acknowledgments

This wildflower guide was originally published in 1976. Many people, knowingly or unknowingly, contributed to this new volume by being helpful and encouraging along the way. They made this book fun to produce. The kindness of these many people is gratefully acknowledged.

Several individuals were extremely helpful in directing me to places where I could photograph specific wildflowers: Chuck Telford directed me to several places in the northern Sierra Nevada. Lillian Mott of Grass Valley pointed me to good wildflower hunting in the Donner Pass area and has remained a good friend. Mary DeDecker suggested good botanizing in the southern Sierra. Forest Service and National Park Service officials were extremely helpful in supplying maps, information, and directions for my explorations. Although most have long since gone on to other assignments, I would again like to extend thanks to them for their help: Edwin Rockwell of the Inyo National Forest, Gordon Heebner and Ted Stubblefield of the Sequoia National Forest, Owen Evans of the Lake Tahoe Basin Management Unit, Bob Fry of Yosemite National Park, and Dick Burns of Sequoia Kings Canyon National Parks. Both National Parks offered their library and herbarium facilities for study and plant identification.

I am especially grateful to Dr. Carl Sharsmith of Yosemite National Park. He graciously shared his knowledge and observances of Sierra flora. I cherish both the many hours we spent in rambling walks in the Tuolumne Meadows area of Yosemite National Park and his friendship in the years until his death.

The late John Thomas Howell of the California Academy of Sciences was kind and gracious in his assistance. He hosted me on several visits, and his suggestions on the original manuscript enhanced it immensely.

Dr. A. A. Lindsey of Purdue University and Dr. Kenton Chambers of Oregon State University kindly consented to read the original manuscript. Their suggestions and aid greatly improved its clarity and readability.

New material was added for this edition of the book, including descriptions and photos of about twenty-five additional species and greatly expanded descriptions of plant families. The nomenclature also has been updated to reflect the changes made in *The Jepson Manual*. I am extremely grateful for the assistance of James R. Shevock, regional botanist for the U.S. Forest Service, for reviewing the manuscript and offering many helpful suggestions. Dr. John Sawyer, Humboldt State University, also reviewed the text, making numerous suggestions that added to its clarity and accuracy.

To all these people, I am most grateful.

INTRODUCTION

The Sierra Nevada

The Sierra Nevada, with its conifer forests, grassy foothills, open rocky vistas, and expanses of magnificent, windy high country, forms a mountain chain along the eastern border of California, crossing into Nevada where the Carson Range lies east of Lake Tahoe. The Sierra Nevada generally lies along a north-south fault line. It is a tilted block that gradually rises in elevation on the western slope and then abruptly drops on the eastern slope to the floor of the Great Basin. Extending nearly four hundred miles, the Sierra Nevada rises gradually southward from Plumas County to Kern County. The elevations of the mountain passes illustrate this rise toward the south. Yuba Pass (6,701 feet elevation), Donner Pass (7,240 feet elevation), Carson Pass (8,573 feet elevation), Tioga Pass (9,941 feet elevation), and Forester Pass (13,300 feet elevation) are examples.

The Sierra Nevada lies in an area that originally laid under the ocean—some 500 million years ago. Sediments collected and hardened to rock. The rocky floor of the sea was uplifted about 150 million years ago and formed a mountain range that was to later become the Sierra Nevada. About 10 million years ago the earth's crust developed faults, along which large blocks of the earth's crust slid, creating many folds and crests in the surface. This landscape was later sculpted by the Ice Age glaciers, some ten thousand years ago; their action formed the broad valleys, knife-edged ridges, triangular peaks, and high country lake basins that characterize the Sierra Nevada today.

Plant Distribution

Plant distribution depends greatly on soil, aspect, elevation, precipitation, and temperature. Because the Sierra Nevada lies in the path of the prevailing Pacific winds, most of the moisture is dropped on the western slope, leaving the eastern slope much drier. In the high country, moisture comes in the form of snow, which as it melts provides a fairly constant supply of water during the growing season. Summers are dry except for occasional thunderstorms. Aridity also increases as one goes southward in the mountain range.

The Sierra flora is a mixture of arctic species that also grow in the Cascade Range and Rocky Mountains, together with plants related to those occurring in the western lowlands and eastern deserts surrounding the Sierra. This is a young mountain range, with extensive alpine areas. The alpine flora consists both of arctic-alpine plants that are found in other mountainous areas across the Northern Hemisphere (mountain sorrel is a good example) and also endemic plants that are found nowhere else in the world (sky pilot is a good example).

Greatly influenced by the patterns of temperature and precipitation, the vegetation of the Sierra Nevada can generally be grouped into several zones or belts. On the lower western slopes, usually called the foothills, are found shrub lands (chaparral) and mixed oak or pine woodlands. Above the foothills are rich conifer forests, merging at higher elevations with alpine areas, where the growing season is too short and climate too severe to allow a continuous tree cover. These zones also exist on the eastern slope of the Sierra Nevada but as much narrower bands that are altered by drier conditions. On the eastern slope, Sierra plant species intermingle with vegetation from the Great Basin and adjacent desert mountain ranges.

Each of these zones will be described, along with its dominant vegetation.

Foothills Zone. The warm, lower western slopes comprise the foothill zone, whose vegetation consists of grasslands, chaparral growth, and open woodlands extending up to about 5,000 feet elevation. Winters are cool and wet, while summers are hot and dry. Various species of oak, pine, ceanothus, and manzanita locally dominate. Often a colorful display of wildflowers carpets the foothills during the spring, while most plants become dormant in the summer. Only those species that extend into the coniferous forests at higher elevations will be treated in this wildflower guide.

Mixed Conifer Zone. The mixed conifer forest grows between the foothills and the red fir/lodgepole pine forests. It lies at 3,000 to 6,000 feet elevation in the northern Sierra, 4,000 to 7,000 feet elevation in the central, and 5,000 to 8,000 feet elevation in the southern Sierra Nevada. Summer temperatures are warm but not as hot as in the foothill zone, and occasional summer showers bring relief. These luxuriant conifer forests contain a rich mixture of towering trees with spires reaching toward the sky.

Sometimes referred to as the montane forest or transition zone, the lower elevations of this zone are characterized by ponderosa pine *(Pinus ponderosa)*, sugar pine *(P. lambertiana),* and, in drier sites, Jeffrey pine *(P. jeffreyi).* Douglas fir *(Pseudotsuga menziesii)* becomes more important in the northern Sierra. Sugar pine, Jeffrey pine, and white fir *(Abies concolor)* are often plentiful in the upper part of the zone. White fir is most often found on the moister, north-facing slopes and may form almost pure stands near the upper part of the zone. Incense cedar *(Calocedrus decurrens)* is also prominent. Both white fir and incense cedar are more prominent in today's Sierra than they were in the 1800s. When fire repeatedly burned lightly over the forest floor, more open, ponderosa pine forests dominated Sierran slopes. The exclusion of fire allowed additional species.

The giant sequoia *(Sequoiadendron giganteum)* forms groves at the mid to upper portion of this zone up to altitudes of about 6,800 feet. Extending from the central Sierra southward, it grows best in the southern Sierra, especially in the Giant Forest and Mountain Home areas of Tulare County.

Many showy and colorful shrubs also grow in the mixed conifer forest. Typical understory shrubs include Sierra gooseberry *(Ribes roezlii),* thimble-

A seep near Stony Creek in the mixed conifer forest along General's Highway, Sequoia Kings Canyon National Park

Giant sequoia in Wawona Grove, Yosemite National Park

An open lodgepole pine woodland along May Lake Trail, Yosemite National Park

berry *(Rubus parviflorus)*, and mountain misery *(Chamaebatia foliolosa)*. Greenleaf manzanita *(Arctostaphylos patula)* and deerbrush *(Ceanothus integerrimus)* are common components of the forest and extend into the foothill chaparral.

Red Fir/Lodgepole Pine Zone. This forest is extensive in the Sierra Nevada and contains a wide variety of plant species. Depending on latitude, it is found between 6,500 and 8,500 feet elevation. The red fir/lodgepole pine forest is controlled by a cool climate and short growing season due to typically long, snowy winters and dry summers. Although the summer daytime temperatures may be warm, temperatures can drop below freezing on any night. There may be afternoon thundershowers during the summer.

Red fir *(Abies magnifica)*, elegantly described by John Muir as "charmingly symmetrical," is the most important and extensive species found in this forest zone. It typically grows in dense stands to the exclusion of other species and dominates large areas of the Sierra forest. While red fir thrives in gravelly soil or slopes of deep rocky soils, lodgepole pine *(Pinus contorta)* grows along the edges of wet meadows or in areas that are well drained. It also forms extensive tracts all the way to timberline. Sparse stands of western white pine *(Pinus monticola)* and Jeffrey pine *(P. jeffreyii)* are scattered throughout the zone, intermingled with red fir. White fir *(Abies concolor)* is common in the lower elevations of the zone, and mountain hemlock *(Tsuga mertensiana)* extends toward timberline.

A wide variety of flowering shrubs and wildflowers inhabit the shady forest and sunny openings. Shrubby members of the forest flora include spirea *(Spirea densiflora)*, serviceberry *(Amelanchier alnifolia)*, wax currant *(Ribes cereum)*, and whitethorn *(Ceanothus cordulatus)*. The deep shade shelters prince's pine *(Chimaphila umbellata)*, white-veined pyrola *(Pyrola picta)*, pinedrops *(Pterospora andromedea)*, spotted coralroot *(Corallorhiza maculata)*, and stripped coralroot *(C. striata)*. Colorful herbaceous wildflowers are abundant in small openings and include cassiope *(Cassiope mertensiana)*, red heather *(Phyllodoce breweri)*, meadow penstemon *(Penstemon heterodoxus)*, columbine *(Aquilegia pubescens)*, scarlet gilia *(Ipomopsis aggregata)*, and elephant's head *(Pedicularis groenlandica)*.

Subalpine and Alpine Zones. Timberline falls near 7,000 feet elevation in the northern Sierra and near 11,000 feet elevation in the southern part of the range. Above timberline is the alpine zone, with its open, rocky expanses and both wet and dry meadows. Deep blankets of snow cover the ground through much of the year, and the growing season is a scant two months long, with occasional summer thunderstorms. Summer temperatures are moderate but days are rarely very warm. Frost or snow can come at any time during the summer. Because the atmosphere is thin, sunlight is very intense.

The most common conifers of the subalpine forest and extending into the alpine areas at and above timberline are the whitebark pine *(Pinus albicaulis)*, lodgepole pine *(P. contorta)*, mountain hemlock *(Tsuga mertensiana)*, juniper *(Juniperus occidentalis)*, and, toward the south, foxtail pine *(P. balfouriana)*. Whitebark pine grows widely spaced on protected slopes. Mountain hemlock mingles with lower-elevation red fir but is often the dominant tree species

Subalpine forests thin and become sparse at higher elevations in Yosemite National Park.

Small groves of trees at the headwaters of the Tuolumne River punctuate this timberline meadow.

The dry, open eastern slopes of the Sierra Nevada at Onion Valley, Inyo National Forest

near timberline in the southern Sierra. The stately lodgepole pine of lower elevations appears here as a weathered shrub or mat.

Many subalpine and alpine herbaceous plants grow as low mats. Typical low-growing plants include raillardella *(Raillardella argentea)*, daisy *(Erigeron compositus)*, timberline phacelia *(Phacelia hastata)*, sky pilot *(Polemonium eximium)*, Sierra primrose *(Primula suffrutescens)*, rock fringe *(Epilobium obcordatum)*, mountain sorrel *(Oxygia digyna)*, and alpine gold *(Hulsea algida)*.

The alpine meadows, while more extensive than in the Cascade Mountains to the north, where they occur only on the highest peaks, are not continuous throughout the Sierra. Numerous gaps or passes that cut the crest of the range dip below the elevation required for the alpine zone. For instance, the continuity of the alpine zone is broken for about 3 miles at Tioga Pass. The crest is interrupted for nearly 20 miles at Mammoth Pass (about 25 miles south of Tioga Pass). In the northern Sierra the alpine zone is more restricted. Nonetheless, particularly in the central and southern Sierra Nevada, there are many extensive alpine areas, bordered by subalpine forest that interjects fingers of trees where conditions allow.

Eastern Slope. The eastern slope of the Sierra is much more precipitous than the western slope. Although it has similar zones, these are greatly condensed due to the smaller area and more abrupt change in elevation. This is relatively apparent, for example, if you drive the short distance between Tioga Pass and Lee Vining. On the eastern slope, the red fir forest is found in the Carson Range east of Lake Tahoe and in local areas of the northern Sierra. The lodgepole pine forest is represented mostly by small patches. Jeffrey pine is the most important species of the mixed conifer forest represented on the eastern slope. Woodlands of pinyon pine *(Pinus monophylla)* and juniper *(Juniperus occidentalis)* represent the foothill zone. Bitterbrush *(Purshia tridentata)*, big sagebrush *(Artemisia tridentata)*, and rubber rabbitbrush *(Chrysothamnus nauseosus)* are found in the scrub zone, although these species also extend nearly to timberline. Joshua trees *(Yucca brevifolia)* grow in canyons along the eastern slopes of the southern Sierra, especially in the Walker Pass area.

Habitats

Exploring the natural communities of the Sierra Nevada can be a stimulating and enjoyable pastime. The place where a plant (or animal) lives is called its habitat. This can refer to the particular surroundings or a combination of factors. A forest, a wet meadow, a stream bank, or a rocky slope are all examples of habitats.

Observing the habitat where a plant grows can be very helpful because you will learn that where you find some types of plants, certain other plants will be nearby. Keep this in mind as you travel the Sierra Nevada. A great variety of habitats exist throughout the foothill, mixed conifer, red fir/lodgepole pine, subalpine, alpine, and eastern slope zones.

Forests. Shaded or partially shaded conifer forests harbor many wildflowers that must have shelter from intense temperature changes and drying wind

A forest edge in Plumas National Forest
provides sunny and shady habitats.
Wet habitat along Bishop Creek,
Inyo National Forest

Dry, open habitat in Yosemite National Park

Alpine habitat above Winnemucca Lake,
north of Carson Pass

and sunlight. The white-veined pyrola *(Pyrola picta)*, rattlesnake plantain *(Goodyera oblongifolia)*, wild ginger *(Asarum hartwegii)*, false Solomon's seal *(Smilacina racemosa)*, and violet *(Viola* species) are good examples of plants most often encountered in shaded forests.

Dry Habitats. Forest openings, rocky bluffs, sunny roadsides, forest borders, and dry meadows are examples of areas inhabited by plants requiring well-drained soil. These openings occur in all the forested zones of the Sierra, and many species growing on mid-elevation rocky slopes also inhabit similar areas at timberline. The manzanita *(Arctostaphylos* species), stonecrop *(Sedum* species), and penstemon *(Penstemon* species) are examples of wildflowers requiring warm, dry sites.

Wet Habitats. Wet and moist meadows, streams, pond margins, and damp swales are special areas found in every zone of the Sierra. Since much of the Sierra Nevada is seasonally dry, water exerts a profound influence. Streams, for instance, may have lush vegetation along their banks, while the forest floor a few feet away lacks herbaceous cover. Wet areas, whether in sunny openings or within shaded woodlands, often have a greater variety of wildflowers than any other. Elephanthead *(Pedicularis groenlandica)*, ladies' tresses *(Spiranthes romanzoffiana)*, camas *(Camassia quamash)*, monkshood *(Aconitum columbianum)*, marsh marigold *(Caltha leptosepala)*, bistort *(Polygonum bistortoides)*, and corn lily *(Veratrum californicum)* are a few of the flowers found in these areas.

Alpine Habitats. The plants growing above timberline are usually low-growing and matted. Rocky slopes, low swales with long-lasting snowbanks, streams draining melting snowfields, and rugged terrain are all components of the Sierran alpine habitat. Low-growing, ground-hugging plants residing here include such colorful wildflowers as draba *(Draba lemmonii)*, rock fringe *(Epilobium obcordatum)*, daisy *(Erigeron compositus)*, timberline phacelia *(Phacelia hastata)*, and phlox *(Phlox diffusa)*.

How to Use This Book

Sierra Nevada Wildflowers will help you identify many of the flowering plants you will find as you travel throughout the Sierra Nevada. This book describes more than 300 species of wildflowers and flowering shrubs and includes more than 225 color photographs. Although identifying wildflowers can be difficult, especially for the novice, the book's photographs coupled with the plant descriptions should make plant identification fun.

The plants described in this book are grouped by family, and the families are organized alphabetically by common name. Within each family, the plants are listed alphabetically by genus name so you can more easily compare related plants. This strict alphabetization is violated in a few places to facilitate the matching of photographs with descriptions. A description of the general characteristics of each family precedes the individual plant profiles and will help you associate flowers that look similar to each other. As you become familiar with some members of a family, the family resemblance will help you recognize other members of that family.

The plant profiles include information about the size, flower color, blooming period, and leaf type. In many cases, you will also find information on historic uses of the plant, derivation of the scientific name, similar species, and specific locations in the Sierra Nevada where you can expect to find the plant. Technical terminology has been kept to a minimum, and the illustrated glossary (page 203) defines the botanical terms that have been used.

The floral descriptions include information about where the plants grow—their habitats—so take notice of a plant's environment. Is it growing in a rocky crevice? On a gravelly slope? Along a rushing stream? Alongside a retreating snowbank? On a riverbank? In the shade of a red fir or lodgepole pine? By noting the habitat of the plants you identify, you will soon anticipate finding additional specimens in similar areas when you travel elsewhere in the Sierra Nevada.

The floral descriptions also include the range or geographic distribution of the plant. Is it found in the entire Sierra Nevada or just the southern part of the range? Does it grow elsewhere in California? Plants from the higher elevations of the Sierra Nevada likely inhabit other mountain ranges, such as the Cascade Range or the Rocky Mountains. Combining the overall distribution of the plant with its habitat will tell you a lot about the species and help you recognize it when you next encounter it.

To make your hike or picnic in the Sierra Nevada even more interesting, try getting acquainted with the book before your outing. Then take this little book with you as you travel the winding roadsides through the foothills or the spectacular travelways through the high Sierra Nevada passes. Keep this book handy in your day pack or overnight packsack as you trek along a trail leading to windblown peaks or mountain lakes. Stop along the way to look at the wildflowers that enhance the scenery. Knowing a little about them and their names will make your Sierra Nevada visits more rewarding and fun.

Scientific Names and Common Names

Most wildflowers have more than one common name, depending on where they grow, their medicinal or functional use, or a variety of other factors. Therefore common names are often quite confusing. Even the beginning botanist should attempt to learn the scientific names of plants, simply because the scientific name is more likely to be standardized. Plant names listed in this guide follow those in *The Jepson Manual: Higher Plants of California.*

A good example of a plant with many common names depending on location is *Lilium washingtonianum*. In northern California it is called the Shasta lily; in northern Oregon it is called the Mount Hood lily. The names cat's ear, sego lily, mariposa lily, and star tulip are all used for members of the genus *Calochortus*, and these names are often used interchangeably. The names skyrocket, foxfire, and scarlet gilia all designate the same wildflower. There are many such examples. But *Oxyria digyna* refers to a single species, whether it grows in the Sierra, the Rocky Mountains, or in the northern mountains of Europe or Asia. This plant's common name is mountain sorrel.

Two words make up the scientific name of every plant. The first is the genus name, the second is the descriptive specific epithet. In our example, *Oxyria* is the genus name. The full name is *Oxyria digyna*. These words are often derived from Greek or Latin names and may, therefore, seem strange to us. Nonetheless, they often tell us something about the particular plant. The name *Oxyria*, for instance, comes from the Greek *oxys,* which means "sharp or sour" and refers to the acid juice that gives the plant a sharp, acidic taste. Often names are descriptive, such as *triphylla,* which means "three leaves," *occidentalis,* which means "western," or *striata,* which means "striped." Some names commemorate a famous botanist or naturalist. *Purshia tridentata* is the scientific name for bitterbrush. *Purshia* honors an early American botanist, Frederick Pursh. The name *tridentata* describes the three-toothed leaf tip.

Sierra Nevada Wildflowers

BELLFLOWER FAMILY   Campanulaceae

The bellflower family is a cosmopolitan group containing some two thousand species. They extend from temperate and subtropical areas into colder climates and mountainous zones. The family contains many beautiful wildflowers as well as cultivated ornamentals. The flowers have floral parts in fives. Often the petals fuse to form a tube. The cardinal flower, balloon-flower, and canterbury bells are good examples.

California Harebell   *Campanula prenanthoides*

Also called bellflower, this delightful little wildflower is easily glimpsed in the shafts of light penetrating sequoia groves and ponderosa pine forests. It has erect, simple stems that have most of their leaves on the lower half. The flowers appear at the top of the stems, first as pale blue, oblong buds, then as blossoms with five reflexed floral lobes. Although the stems occasionally reach 3 feet in length, they are usually only about 10 to 20 inches tall. This delicate little flower blooms from June to September.

Found in the Sierra Nevada north into southern Oregon.

BORAGE FAMILY   Boraginaceae

The borage family consists mainly of herbs that are hairy or bristly, with flowers typically in coiled clusters and floral parts in fives. Common garden plants belonging to this group include the heliotrope, hound's-tongue, stickseed, and forget-me-not.

Stickseed   *Hackelia velutina*

Stickseeds, also known as sticktights and beggarticks, are named for their one-seeded fruits, which have flat, barbed prickles, allowing them easy attachment to passersby. Stickseeds have alternate, narrow leaves without teeth or lobes. The flowers are five-lobed and form a short tube with five scales at the throat. Many of the characteristics that determine the species deal with fruits, but the stickseed group itself is fairly easy to recognize.

Hackelia velutina grows 12 to 24 inches tall and is a somewhat hairy or velvety textured plant. The basal leaves are oblong, from 2 to 4 inches long. The stem leaves are lanceolate, gradually reduced in size toward the upper part of the stem. The pink or blue flowers are about a half-inch across. When a plant first starts to bloom, the flower clusters are tightly coiled; as they unfurl, they take on a loosely ragged, open appearance. Stickseed blooms from June to early August on dry open woodlands and is rather common at moderate elevations.

Found in the Cascades and Sierra Nevada.

Similar species: *Hackelia nervosa* is very similar. It grows through most of the Sierra Nevada and has a rough-hairy texture and quarter-inch blue flowers. A stickseed bearing a small white or blue flower with a yellow center, ***Hackelia sharsmithii*** grows in subalpine and alpine sites around Mount Whitney. It grows only 4 to 12 inches tall. ***Hackelia micrantha*** is also a hairy plant, growing 12 to 24 inches tall. It has pale blue flowers and is common in moist places at moderate elevations.

California Harebell   *Campanula prenanthoides*

Stickseed   *Hackelia velutina*   Stickseed   *Hackelia velutina*

Streamside Bluebells
Mertensia ciliata

Bluebells are also called languid ladies because of their drooping leaves and flower clusters. As a group, bluebells have smooth, alternate leaves that are sometimes covered with fine hairs, giving them a bluish cast. The nodding, tubular flowers are quite showy. Bluebells grow up to 5 feet tall with stems clustered together to give the appearance of a bush or shrub from a distance. The half-inch flowers are pale pink in bud, turning blue as they mature, and fading to pink again.

Streamside bluebells grow in damp areas, such as wet meadows or stream banks, usually associated with willow, butterweed, and monkeyflowers. They bloom from June to August.

Found in the Sierra Nevada north into Oregon and east into Nevada, Utah, and Montana.

BUCKEYE FAMILY
Hippocastanaceae

The buckeye family is a small group of plants, containing fewer than twenty species, mostly in the Northern Hemisphere. The family contains shrubs or small trees with showy plumes of flowers.

California Buckeye
Aesculus californica

The California buckeye is a shrub or small tree that can be found blooming in the Sierra foothills. It is conspicuous along the Ash Mountain Road into Sequoia Kings Canyon National Park. It grows 30 to 40 feet high and is entirely covered by finger-shaped clusters of white or pale pink flowers in May and June. The showy flower clusters are 6 to 8 inches long and contain tubular flowers with flared lobes. The flowers are replaced by glossy, brown seeds later in the summer. The large leaves are palmately compound, each leaflet being about 6 inches long. They are shed in early summer as soon as the soil dries.

California buckeye seeds are toxic; American Indians used them to poison pools and streams, making fish easy to catch. However, after thorough leaching and soaking, the seeds could be used as food.

Found widely at lower elevations in California.

Streamside Bluebells *Mertensia ciliata*

Streamside Bluebells *Mertensia ciliata*   California Buckeye *Aesculus californica*

BUCKTHORN FAMILY Rhamnaceae

The buckthorn family contains many trees, shrubs, and a few woody vines, with some nine hundred species. The genus *Ceanothus,* or California lilac, is included in this family and grows mostly in the foothills and mountains of the western United States. California has more than forty species of *Ceanothus,* with about ten in the Sierra. *Ceanothus* species are usually upright shrubs, although a few are prostrate. Some have spiny branches but most do not. As a group, *Ceanothus* is not difficult to recognize. The blue or white flowers form showy clusters. When these are on the tips of the branches, they are especially spectacular. The five petals of each flower are spoon-shaped, with a thin, inrolled throat and hoodlike tip. The leaves typically have three prominent ribs or veins on the lower side.

The genus *Ceanothus* contains fragrant, attractive shrubs. Many horticulturalists have added them to home, garden, and park landscaping. Many natural hybrids occur. They are also important components of the foothill plant community. They respond readily to periodic fires by resprouting from underground stems, making them an important part of any chaparral community.

Whitethorn *Ceanothus cordulatus*

Also called snowbush, this lovely ceanothus has white flowers in small, dense, round-topped clusters about 1 or 2 inches long, which bloom from May through July. Whitethorn is a flat-topped, densely branched shrub that grows 1 to 4 feet high and 3 to 9 feet across. Its leaves are alternate on the stems and have three prominent veins. Another distinctive characteristic is the hard point or "thorn" found at the tips of most branches. Whitethorn commonly dominates areas that have been repeatedly burned, sharing the site with greenleaf manzanita (see page 66). It grows in open ponderosa pine forests and upper elevations in the Sierra.

Found in many mountainous areas of California north into Oregon, east into Nevada, and south into Baja California.

Similar species: Chaparral whitethorn *(Ceanothus leucodermis)* commonly grows in sandy or rocky soil in foothill areas. Its gray, spiny, rigid branches carry smooth, ovate leaves and pale blue or white flowers in 1- to 3-inch clusters. The leaves are alternate on the branches and have three prominent veins. Chaparral whitethorn grows 5 to 12 feet tall and blooms from April to June. **Wedgeleaf ceanothus** or **buckbrush *(Ceanothus cuneatus)*** may be prostrate or upright, perhaps growing 3 to 12 feet high. It is a many-branched shrub with thick, wedge-shaped, evergreen leaves in opposite pairs along the stem. Buckbrush blooms from March to May, the small white to blue flowers forming an umbrella-shaped cluster up to 1 inch across. Most often found on dry, gravelly slopes and ridges in the foothills, where it often forms extensive thickets, buckbrush also grows in rocky openings within ponderosa pine forests.

Whitethorn *Ceanothus cordulatus*

Deerbrush
Ceanothus integerrimus

Deerbrush, named because deer often browse the foliage, is one of the most common species of *Ceanothus* in the Sierra. Its thin, oval leaves are about 2 inches long and alternate on the stem. Deerbrush grows 4 to 12 feet high and has fragrant flowers in showy 2- to 6-inch-wide terminal clusters of tiny blue or white flowers. Deerbrush is extremely common in openings and partial shade at lower and moderate elevations, blooming from April to July.

Found in California and Arizona north to Washington and Nevada.

Mahala Mat
Ceanothus prostratus

This delightful buckthorn, also called squaw carpet, is readily recognized by its hollylike evergreen leaves, which form a prostrate mat covering the ground. The trailing branches frequently root and form a dense ground cover 2 to 10 feet across; sometimes it extends over an even larger area. The stiff leaves are about 1 inch long, and small blue flowers bloom at the ends of the twigs from April to May.

This low-growth form protects the soil from erosion and provides a nurse-bed for young conifers. Douglas fir and white fir benefit from mahala mat, which protects their seeds from rodents. It also provides shade and helps hold moisture, creating a more favorable condition for seedlings than hot, open mountain slopes.

Found in the northern Sierra into Washington and Idaho.

Similar species: Fresno mat *(Ceanothus fresnensis)* also forms prostrate mats, although it may have some erect stems. The half-inch long, dark green leaves are leathery, evergreen, and finely toothed. Found at moderate and lower elevations in the central and southern Sierra, the blue flowers bloom in May and June. **Littleleaf ceanothus** *(C. parvifolius)* rarely exceeds 3 feet in height. Its elliptic leaves, however, are deciduous and have smooth edges. The pale or deep blue flower clusters bloom from June to July in lodgepole and ponderosa pine forests.

Tobacco Bush
Ceanothus velutinus

Tobacco bush is one of the most widespread members of the *Ceanothus* genus, occurring in the Rocky Mountains, Sierra Nevada, and Cascade Range. It also has a wide altitudinal range, growing from the foothills nearly to timberline. Usually forming small patches or extensive brushfields, it does well in a variety of situations and exposures. It has large, shiny, evergreen leaves, which may be 3 inches long. They are three-ribbed at the base and somewhat sticky to touch. This trait accounts for another of its common names, sticky laurel. Averaging 2 to 5 feet tall, tobacco bush has white, sweetly scented flowers borne in showy clusters from 1 to 4 inches long.

Found widely in the mountains of the western states.

Deerbrush *Ceanothus integerrimus*

Mahala Mat *Ceanothus prostratus*
Tobacco Bush *Ceanothus velutinus*

Buckwheat Family Polygonaceae

The buckwheat family is worldwide in distribution and contains some one thousand species. Most species are herbaceous, although a few are shrubby or are small trees. Generally, the plant stems are swollen at the nodes (the place on the stems where the leaves attach). The leaves are entire or slightly lobed, occasionally toothed or cleft. The floral arrangements vary and include spikes, cymes, racemes, or panicles. The flowers are somewhat unique in that they lack petals. The buckwheat family contains some important food sources, including buckwheat, which is raised extensively in many parts of the world, and rhubarb.

BUCKWHEATS *Eriogonum* species

More than one hundred species of *Eriogonum* grow in California. As a group they are fairly easy to recognize. Always found in dry areas, their short, woody stems produce many branches that run along the surface of the ground and have clusters of linear or oval leaves at their tips. These leaves are always entire—meaning the edges have no teeth or lobes—and often have a covering of woolly hairs on at least one surface. The flowering stalks have only a few leaves, or in some species, none at all. The flowers form tight balls or clusters, arranged in a terminal umbel at the end of the flowering stems.

Marum-Leaved Eriogonum *Eriogonum marifolium*

This eriogonum is a loosely branched plant with woody stems and, at 4 to 16 inches high, resembles a miniature shrub. The rounded, ovate leaves are low to the ground and are green on the upper surface but covered with short, white hairs on the underside. The flowers are pale yellow, tinged with red, and found in round, terminal clusters at the ends of the stems. This eriogonum is fairly common, growing in dry, gravelly, or sandy places at middle to upper elevations. It can be found within the red fir forest and into subalpine areas.

Found from the central Sierra Nevada north into Oregon and Nevada.

Nude Buckwheat *Eriogonum nudum*

Nude buckwheat is distinctive because of the 1- to 3-foot-tall, leafless stems. The leaves are clustered at the base of the stem or occasionally on the lower portion of the stem. The small, white flowers, usually tinged with pink or yellow, are crowded into a ball-shaped cluster at the tips of the tall stems or, if the stems branch, in the fork of the stems. This buckwheat inhabits sandy or gravelly spots from the foothills to subalpine areas. Watch for it in the sunny openings alongside roadways.

Found in the Sierra north to Washington and Nevada, also in the southern Rocky Mountains.

Marum-Leaved Eriogonum *Eriogonum marifolium*

Nude Buckwheat *Eriogonum nudum*

Oval-Leaved Eriogonum   *Eriogonum ovalifolium*

Oval-leaved eriogonum is a species that may grow in windswept timber-line areas or at moderate elevations throughout the Sierra Nevada. It is a densely matted plant, with small, half-inch leaves crowded together on short, basal shoots. The oval leaves are covered on both surfaces with soft, woolly, white hairs, reminiscent of a piece of felt. The flowering stems are only a few inches tall and carry balls of tiny, cream-colored flowers, which are often tinted with red.

Found in the mountains of California, north in the mountains to south-ern Canada and Montana, east into the Rocky Mountains.

Similar species: Frosty eriogonum *(Eriogonum incanum)* grows as a low, matted plant that may be several feet across. The short stems are 2 to 10 inches tall. Both the leaves and stems are covered with dense, white hairs, giving the plant a cushiony effect. The pale yellow flowers form rounded clusters. It grows in well-drained soils at higher elevations in the Sierra Nevada.

Sulphur-Flower   *Eriogonum umbellatum*

Of the many wild buckwheats found in the Sierra Nevada, sulphur-flower is one of the most common and conspicuous. It is fairly abundant in dry, rocky places, both in the cliffs and openings of pine and red fir forests of moderate elevations and in the high country near timberline. Sulphur-flower is easy to spot: the bright yellow or sulphur-colored flowers form tight, umbrella-like clusters above a compact mat of leafy stems covering the ground. As the flowers mature they become red or pink, the dried remains turning completely brown by the end of the summer. The flower clusters are on short stalks, 4 to 12 inches tall, that rise from a many-branched woody base. Shorter, flowerless stems have small, spatulate leaves.

Found in the mountains of California north into western Canada and also in the Rocky Mountains.

Oval-Leaved Eriogonum *Eriogonum ovalifolium*

Sulphur-Flower *Eriogonum umbellatum*

Mountain Sorrel
Oxyria digyna

Recognize this delicate, alpine perennial by the smooth, round or kidney-shaped basal leaves that emerge from a woody base. The green or reddish flowers are only a quarter-inch long and hang from the tip of the upright, 2- to 10-inch-tall stems. The thin, flat fruits are also conspicuous, being a deep rose color.

A plant that is widely distributed in the mountains of the western United States, mountain sorrel is well known to most hikers and campers who venture above timberline. Found nestled on rocky slopes between 4,000 and 13,000 feet elevation, it is confined to moist crevices that protect it from drying, gusty winds. We often think of the windswept alpine zone as being desertlike, but slow-melting snowbanks provide a constant supply of moisture, and irregular topography creates shelter for a variety of plants. You might look for alpine sorrel when you're hiking along the rocky alpine expanses around Piute Pass and Tioga Pass in late July and August.

The generic name *Oxyria* is derived from a Greek word meaning "sour," and refers to the acidic juice of the leaves. Hikers find mountain sorrel leaves a refreshing snack.

Found from Alaska to Greenland, southward on the higher mountains of North America. This is a circumpolar species, also growing in the mountains of Europe and Asia.

American Bistort
Polygonum bistortoides

The flowers of this member of the buckwheat family, also called western bistort or mountain knotweed, are conspicuous components of the meadow community at Crane Flat in Yosemite National Park, Haypress Meadows in the Desolation Wilderness of the Eldorado National Forest, and Onion Valley of the Inyo National Forest. The white or pinkish flowers are compacted into a dense, oblong cluster atop a 10- to 24-inch stalk. These stems grow from a large, fleshy rootstock that survives from year to year. Most of the long, narrow leaves are at the base of the plant and are from 4 to 10 inches long. A few shorter leaves, however, may be found along the length of the stem. Flowering from June through August, American bistort grows in wet meadows at middle elevations and in upper-elevation forests.

American bistort grows in a variety of areas within western North America. In the Rocky Mountains it inhabits the alpine and subalpine areas. It also grows in scattered areas along the Pacific coast. In the Sierra Nevada it characteristically grows in subalpine areas, rarely at timberline as it so often does in the Cascades. The plants found in these widespread areas differ in many subtle ways. Those in the Sierra Nevada, for instance, reproduce mainly by the spreading of underground rootstocks, while those in the Rockies reproduce from seed.

Although the young leaves can be used as greens, the bistort root was the more important food for American Indians in the region, who used it in soups and stews.

Found widely in western North America, east across the northern continent to the Atlantic.

Mountain Sorrel *Oxyria digyna*

American Bistort *Polygonum bistortoides*

BUTTERCUP FAMILY   Ranunculaceae

The buttercup family is found worldwide, especially in the Northern Hemisphere. It contains such attractive ornamentals as the anemone, larkspur, columbine, and globeflower. Several medicinal plants are also in this family, including snakeroot and goldenseal. The family includes herbaceous perennials and annuals as well as a few shrubs and vines. The leaves are usually alternate and flowers are usually symmetrical, although in some species various petals or sepals form extended spurs or hoods.

Monkshood   *Aconitum columbianum*

This member of the buttercup family bears little resemblance to the golden flower for which the family is named. Nonetheless, monkshood is distinctive and easy to recognize. Usually an erect plant growing 3 to 4 feet tall, it can be recognized by the tall stems, palmately lobed leaves, and peculiar flower shape. Located near the tip of the stems is the showy flower of deep blue or purple (occasional white specimens have been found). There are five outer flower parts called sepals. The upper one forms a hood. It is this hood-shaped cap that gives the flower its common name.

You will find monkshood throughout the Sierra, although it rarely grows in great abundance in any one place. It inhabits moist meadows and streamsides and is also found in damp, open woods. North Lake Campground in the Inyo National Forest and the damp meadows of the Desolation Wilderness near Lake Tahoe in the Eldorado National Forest are only a few of the places you should expect to see it.

Monkshood may be confused with the larkspur (see page 30). Both grow in similar areas, and the leaves tend to resemble each other. However, the larkspur flower has one sepal forming a spur instead of a hood. Monkshood leaves may resemble those of a geranium (see page 60), making these two plants difficult to tell apart when not in bloom. The crushed leaves of the geranium, though, have a very distinctive odor.

Found in the mountainous regions of the western United States and north into British Columbia.

Baneberry   *Actaea rubra*

This perennial herb has an erect stem 1 to 3 feet tall with large leaves divided three times. The white flowers are in a round-topped cluster at the tip of the stems and have a dainty appearance, largely because of the long, slender stamens. Actually, the fruits or berries are almost as conspicuous as the flowers. They are a bright, shiny red or white, the latter form correctly deserving the common name doll's eyes.

Baneberry can be found in moist woodlands. In the southern Sierra, for instance, in the Mineral King drainage in Sequoia National Park, it blooms in May and June. Farther north it blooms later in the season. Mid-July will find its flowers in the shaded forests around Harden Lake and Morrison Creek in Yosemite National Park. The shiny berries appear about a month after the flowers and are very poisonous.

Found widely in North America.

Monkshood   *Aconitum columbianum*   Monkshood   *Aconitum columbianum*

Baneberry   *Actaea rubra*   Baneberry fruits   *Actaea rubra*

Western Pasqueflower
Anemone occidentalis

Only if you venture into the Sierra high country will you find the blooms of this member of the buttercup family. This striking anemone flowers as soon as the snow melts. The conspicuous white or pale purple flower is almost 2 inches wide and sits atop a stout, hairy stem only a few inches tall. As the plant matures the stem elongates to 12 inches or more. By midsummer the fruiting head of filamentous, feathery tassels has appeared, giving rise to another common name, old man of the mountain. Actually, the tassels look more like a mophead than an old man's mane! Basal leaves are long-stalked, 2 to 4 inches wide, and divided into narrow lobes. You'll find it blooming in July and August on well-drained, rocky slopes.

Found in the high mountains of California north in the Cascades to British Columbia and east into Montana.

Similar species: The closely related **Drummond's anemone *(Anemone drummondii)*** grows in the central and northern Sierra Nevada. Like the pasqueflower, it prefers dry, rocky slopes. The sepals forming the flower are shorter, less than 1 inch long. The main difference in the two plants becomes obvious after the fruit has formed. This anemone lacks the feathery tails that characterize the fruit of the pasqueflower. The fruiting head more closely resembles a woolly globe than a mophead.

Columbine
Aquilegia formosa

One of the most common, best known, and most widely distributed of the native western columbines, *Aquilegia formosa* is also one of our most beautiful wildflowers. The showy flowers nod atop a 2- to 4-foot-tall stem. Five elongated petals are turned backward and upward, forming crimson red spurs, while the forward portions form yellow blades. This columbine may be found from sea level to timberline in the Pacific states. Associated with a wide variety of soil types, it grows particularly well along stream banks, near springs and ponds, in woodland openings, and on moist mountain slopes. The colorful blossoms may be found from May to August, depending on elevation and latitude.

Found widely in the Pacific states and also east to Montana.

Similar species: A columbine found at timberline and windy mountain passes, **Coville's columbine *(Aquilegia pubescens)*** has large yellow to white flowers. Forsaking the sheltered areas preferred by *Aquilegia formosa,* this columbine grows on rocky talus slopes such as those found on the flanks of Mount Dana in Yosemite National Park and along the trail to Piute Pass in the Inyo National Forest. Reflecting more stringent growing conditions at these higher elevations, it is a much smaller plant and grows 6 to 18 inches tall. Where found near each other, these two species tend to hybridize.

Western Pasqueflower
Anemone occidentalis

Western Pasqueflower fruiting head
Anemone occidentalis

Columbine *Aquilegia formosa*

Colville's Columbine *Aquilegia pubescens*

Marsh Marigold   *Caltha leptosepala*

Marsh marigolds have a worldwide reputation for their beauty and as harbingers of spring. The glossy round or kidney-shaped green leaves and the pure white flowers with yellow centers create a strikingly clean appearance as they push up through the snow at the edge of retreating snowbanks. The leaves may be 2 to 4 inches across, while the flower itself is more than 1 inch in diameter. The stout, 4- to 12-inch-tall stems arise from a fibrous rootstock that is invariably anchored in wet meadows, pond margins, or marshy slopes from the mixed conifer to the subalpine zones of the Sierra. Marsh marigold blooms May through July depending on elevation. In Yosemite National Park you will find them pushing up through the ground in May at Summit Meadows or in July along the May Lake Trail.

Found at higher elevations in the Sierra Nevada north to Alaska.

Larkspur   *Delphinium glaucum*

Larkspurs are distinctive members of the buttercup family, and the unusual shape of their flowers makes this group easy to recognize. The flowers have five sepals, which are deep purple or blue (or occasionally white). These sepals are larger and more conspicuous than the four petals. The upper sepal is spurred backward and resembles a dunce cap. Larkspur may sometimes be confused with monkshood (see page 26), which also has a distinctively shaped sepal.

Nearly thirty species of larkspurs are native to California. Most are extremely difficult to tell apart. They inhabit dry flats, woodlands, and ridgetops. This species, sometimes called tall mountain larkspur, is one of the few that is easily distinguished. A robust, leafy plant, growing from 3 to 6 feet tall, it is the largest of the Sierra larkspurs. Its round leaves are 3 to 5 inches wide and cleft into five to seven divisions. The flowers are clustered near the upper part of the tall stems. Inhabiting stream banks and wet meadows at moderate and upper elevations, it is conspicuous wherever it occurs.

Found in California north to Alaska and also in the Rocky Mountains.

Water Plantain Buttercup   *Ranunculus alismaefolius*

The buttercups are a large group of wildflowers that are usually found in wet or boggy areas. The flowers are most easily recognized by the shiny yellow petals, usually numbering five. A waxy coating on the petals gives them their glossy sheen.

The five-petaled, golden yellow flowers of this species are about a half-inch across and grow along sluggish streams and in wet meadows. The plant is named for its long, tapering leaves, which resemble those of the common plantain found in most lowland lawns and fields. Most buttercups have leaves that are lobed or otherwise divided; in this species they are entire or, sometimes, shallowly toothed. The leaves are 2 to 5 inches long, the upper leaves being the shortest and narrowest. The leafy stems are erect, somewhat stout, and grow 1 to 2 feet tall. At higher elevations they may not reach a foot in height.

Found widely in California north to British Columbia and Idaho and east to Wyoming and Nevada.

Marsh Marigold *Caltha leptosepala*

Larkspur *Delphinium glaucum*   **Water Plantain Buttercup** *Ranunculus alismaefolius*

Alpine Buttercup
Ranunculus eschscholtzii

Alpine buttercup basks in the sunshine at timberline and above, usually in the meltwater of a retreating snowbank. Growing up to 6 inches tall, its glossy petals are a bright golden yellow. The rounded leaves are deeply three-lobed, with the middle lobe sometimes being further divided. It is the flower, however, that attracts attention. When in bloom, it covers the leaves and is conspicuous, the individual flowers being 1 to 2 inches across. Look for this little buttercup in rocky meadows and alpine fell-fields. It can be found blooming in places like Emerald Lake in the John Muir Wilderness by early July. In areas where the winter lingers and the snow remains longer, this buttercup saves its spurt of growth and flowering until mid-August. Look for it then around Lake Winnemucca in the Eldorado National Forest.

Found in the Sierra Nevada north to Alaska and also in the Rocky Mountains.

Western Buttercup
Ranunculus occidentalis

Western buttercup grows 6 to 24 inches tall and is most often found in moist ground at lower elevations. Its flowers have five to six waxy yellow petals and are nearly 1 inch across. The leaves are mostly basal and deeply cut into three toothed lobes. Western buttercup occupies a variety of habitats, from moist meadows and grassy flats to openings in woodlands and coniferous forests.

Found in the Pacific states, from California to Alaska.

Similar species: Common buttercup *(Ranunculus californicus)* has lower leaves that are long-petioled and divided. The lobes are coarsely toothed. Instead of consistently having five petals, as most buttercups do, these flowers have between five and twenty-two yellow petals. It also grows at lower elevations in grasslands, open woodlands, and evergreen forest openings in much of California, southern Oregon, and Baja California.

Meadow Rue
Thalictrum fendleri

A daintily flowered plant, meadow rue grows in moist soil alongside streams and wet seeps. The leafy stems grow 1 to 3 feet tall, with large leaves that are divided three times. You will find different types of flowers on separate plants: the male flowers, which produce the pollen, are on one plant; the female flowers, where the seeds are produced, are on another. The male flowers are the ones that resemble hanging green tassels, while the female flowers are less spectacular.

Meadow rue grows at middle and upper elevations throughout the Sierra. Look for it along Taylor Creek when you visit the U.S. Forest Service Visitor Center at Lake Tahoe.

Found in California north to Washington, east to Wyoming and Texas.

Alpine Buttercup   *Ranunculus eschscholtzii*   **Western Buttercup**   *Ranunculus occidentalis*

Common Buttercup   *Ranunculus californicus*   **Meadow Rue male flowers**   *Thalictrum fendleri*

CACAO FAMILY   Sterculiaceae

This family of trees and shrubs, containing some seven hundred species, grows principally in the tropics and subtopics. Its members have alternate leaves that are simple or compound and flowers of three to five somewhat united sepals, five (or no) petals, and numerous stamens. One of this family's more interesting members, the chocolate plant, is a small tree native to Central and South America with large woody pods that contain the oily seeds used to make chocolate and cocoa.

Fremontia   *Fremontodendron californicum*

A beautiful display of large, yellow flowers attracts attention to fremontia in spring and early summer. Often found in disturbed places, such as roadcuts or on rocky banks below 6,000 feet elevation, fremontia grows 3 to 12 feet tall. The dull, lemon yellow flowers are a flat, saucer shape, about 2 inches across. The leaves are round, sometimes three-lobed, and 1 to 2 inches long. The shrub is covered by hairs, which may cause irritation if touched.

Fremontia was named for the explorer John C. Fremont, who crossed the Sierra in 1884. During his five expeditions into western North America, Fremont was an avid collector of plants, many of which now bear his name.

Found widely in the chaparral and foothill areas of California, Arizona, and Baja California.

CARROT FAMILY   Apiaceae

The carrot family is large and distinctive. Members of the carrot (sometimes called parsley) family have compound leaves, stems that are usually hollow, and flowers borne in groups called umbels. An umbel resembles an inside-out umbrella, with all the erect ribs (the flower stems) originating from a common point. Depending on the length of these ribs the flower cluster may be rounded or flat on the top. The distinctive umbel immediately identifies this family. Many commercially important plants, including caraway, dill, parsnip, celery, and carrot, belong to this group.

Sierra Angelica   *Angelica lineariloba*

The angelicas are robust members of the carrot family. These erect perennials grow from stout taproots and have large leaves that are divided several times. Although the flowers are small, the floral clusters are large and conspicuous.

Sierra angelica is a stout-stemmed plant growing 2 to 6 feet tall. Its leaves are divided into numerous narrow leaflets, each from 1 to 4 inches long. The white flowers grace the dry slopes of Mineral King Valley of Sequoia National Park.

Found in the central and southern Sierra Nevada.

Similar species: Brewer's angelica *(Angelica breweri)* is similar but has much wider leaflets that are toothed along the margins and often hairy. It grows in the central and northern Sierra and can be found at Crane Flat and the Hetch Hetchy Valley in Yosemite National Park.

Fremontia *Fremontodendron californicum*   Sierra Angelica *Angelica lineariloba*

Fremontia *Fremontodendron californicum*

Cow Parsnip
Heracleum lanatum

One of the most conspicuous of the wild carrots, cow parsnip derives its scientific name very logically. The name *Heracleum,* derived from the name Hercules, refers to the plant's mighty size; *lanatum* refers to the hairy covering found on most of the stem. The stout stems can grow 6 to 9 feet tall, although 4 or 5 feet is more common. Everything about the cow parsnip is large. The flowers cluster in flat-topped heads 5 to 12 inches across. The leaves, which are divided into three deeply toothed leaflets, are also of large proportions. They are 5 to 20 inches across, and their general form reminds one of rhubarb.

Native Americans collected the tender leaves and sweet, aromatic flowering stalks for food in the spring and early summer before the flower clusters opened. Cattle are also fond of cow parsnip because the green foliage is very palatable. In some places extensive grazing has made the plant difficult to find.

Found in moist openings and along stream banks at middle elevations, cow parsnip blooms from May through August. Cow parsnip is widespread in North America and is also found in parts of Siberia.

Yampah
Perideridia bolanderi

Waving its small, rounded clusters of white flowers, yampah may be found in dry openings or washes. It commonly grows along road shoulders, basking in the sunshine created by this artificial opening. A slender, erect plant standing 1 to 3 feet high, its stems carry only a few long leaves. The leaves are 2 to 6 inches long and divided several times into many linear segments, some of which are substantially longer than others. The basal leaves are divided many times, with the divisions of more than one length.

The roots are edible. The tubers (thick, rounded, underground stems) may grow up to 3 inches long and resemble small sweet potatoes. Native Americans used them extensively for food. Captain John Fremont, who crossed California in 1844, reportedly ate yampah, declaring it to be one of the finest of all native roots. Care should always be used when looking for yampah roots to dig, since the plant resembles death camas (see page 100).

These plants are sometimes referred to as Queen Anne's lace. However, that name is better reserved for plants in the genus *Daucus,* the wild carrot. Most passersby consider yampahs to be weeds, and the plant's abundance causes most viewers to ignore them. Sierra meadows enhanced with white flowers toward the latter half of the summer are usually covered by yampah.

Found through the Sierra Nevada north into eastern Oregon, Utah, and Wyoming.

Similar species: Another Sierra yampah *(Perideridia parishii)* grows in wet or drying meadows. It also has small, white flowers in umbrella-like clusters. It differs from *P. bolanderi* in leaf structure, having leaves that are divided into one or two narrow grasslike or threadlike segments.

Cow Parsnip   *Heracleum lanatum*   Cow Parsnip   *Heracleum lanatum*

Yampah   *Perideridia bolanderi*   **Parish's Yampah**   *Perideridia parishii*

Ranger's Buttons   *Sphenosciadium capitellum*

Ranger's buttons, also called button parsley or swamp white heads, resembles cow parsnip. However, its flowers are not clustered in a flat-topped umbel. Instead the tiny, white flowers form dense, fuzzy balls about a half-inch in diameter. The entire umbel is about 4 inches across.

Flowering from July to August, ranger's buttons grows 2 to 5 feet tall at moderate and upper elevations. Look for it along streams and in other moist places.

Found from southern California to northeast Oregon and Idaho.

Dogbane Family   Apocynaceae

The dogbane family contains about two thousand species of plants, mainly residents of tropical areas. Members of this family have milky sap, simple, entire leaves, and flowers in branched clusters. The flowers have five sepals, five somewhat fused petals, five stamens, and two ovaries. Several ornamentals belong to this group, including oleander and plumeria.

Spreading Dogbane   *Apocynum androsaemifolium*

The dogbanes, also known as Indian hemp and Canadian hemp, constitute a small genus of plants that are widely distributed in the western United States. The genus is marked by the opposite, rather thick, ovate leaves, and small, aromatic, bell-shaped flowers.

Spreading dogbane has very fragrant white or pink flowers. The drooping leaves are 1 to 4 inches long and on spreading, reddish stems 8 to 18 inches tall. The leaves are ovate or rounded, dark green above and paler underneath. Spreading dogbane commonly grows on gravelly roadsides in full sunlight. It also inhabits well-drained hillsides and meadows.

Found widely throughout most of western and eastern North America.

Similar species: Indian hemp *(Apocynum cannabinium)* is found in shady spots, has erect, lanceolate leaves, and grows up to 3 feet tall.

Ranger's Buttons
Sphenosciadium capitellum

Spreading Dogbane
Apocynum androsaemifolium

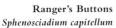

Spreading Dogbane seed capsules and flowers   *Apocynum androsaemifolium*

DOGWOOD FAMILY
Cornaceae

This family contains mostly shrubs and small trees, usually with opposite, simple leaves. The flowering dogwood is a favorite cultivar that graces many yards and gardens.

Mountain Dogwood
Cornus nuttallii

Several species of flowering dogwood grow in western North America. The mountain dogwood is by far the showiest when in bloom. The flowers are extremely small and form green, buttonlike clusters in the center of the large, showy, white bracts, which many people mistake for the flowers. A bract is actually a modified leaf. The mountain dogwood's egg-shaped bracts number four to six for each flower cluster and are 2 to 3 inches long. Flowering normally occurs from April to June, depending on elevation and latitude, with a second flowering in some areas in the fall. The leaves typically turn brilliant red in the fall, rivaling the display of springtime white. The shiny, berrylike red fruits that appear in the fall are also conspicuous, adding color to the autumn forest. John Muir commented that this is when the shrub is most striking, as it becomes "a crimson flame."

Mountain dogwood prefers forested areas and forest edges, where it grows singly or in small groups, especially in moist or damp places. In the Sierra it is common in woodlands dominated by ponderosa or sugar pine.

The generic name *Cornus* comes from the Latin for horn and refers to the hardness of the wood. John James Audubon, the famous ornithologist, named the plant *Cornus nuttallii* in honor of Thomas Nuttall, a naturalist and botanist who visited the West Coast collecting numerous new plant specimens. It was during Nuttall's stay in 1825 at Fort Vancouver on the Columbia River that he distinguished the mountain dogwood of the Pacific from the eastern dogwood, recognizing it as a separate species.

Found through the Pacific states, from California north into Idaho and British Columbia.

American Dogwood
Cornus sericea

This dogwood hardly looks like its larger relative, the mountain dogwood. Instead of growing to the size of a small tree, it remains a shrub, rarely larger than 10 feet tall. Rather than large, showy bracts surrounding the flower cluster, this dogwood has small, white flowers, borne in a round-topped cluster 1 or 2 inches across. Forsaking the shade of forest edges, it abides by streams, sometimes forming dense thickets. One of this dogwood's real beauties is most obvious in the winter, when it and other streamside plants have lost their foliage. American dogwood's winter stems are a deep red color, adding a splash of brightness to any winter setting.

Mountaineers and Indians used the green inner bark of this dogwood as a tobacco substitute.

Found widely across northern North America and southerly in mountainous regions.

Mountain Dogwood   *Cornus nuttallii*

American Dogwood   *Cornus sericea*

EVENING PRIMROSE FAMILY   Onagraceae

Evening primroses are a worldwide family of about 650 species. They are mostly herbaceous plants with simple leaves. The four-petaled flowers are often very showy. Many, such as clarkias, fuchsias, godetias, and evening primroses, are attractive ornamentals.

Farewell to Spring   *Clarkia williamsonii*

Blooming brightly in May, June, and July, this group of wildflowers adds color to otherwise dry openings after the native grasses have turned brown. Several species inhabit the foothill areas and range into the lower conifer forests, adding a splash of color along most of the roads leading into the mountains. Although named for Captain Clark of the famed Lewis and Clark expedition to the mouth of the Columbia River in 1804–6, more *Clarkia* species—more than forty species in all—grow in California than in the Northwest. The genus *Clarkia* has four-petaled pink or purple flowers.

    Common in the foothills and lower forest areas, *Clarkia williamsonii* has purple fan-shaped flower petals that are lighter near the center, with an especially dark purple splotch along the upper edge. The plant's erect stems are about 12 inches tall and have linear leaves. The species name of this *Clarkia* honors Lieutenant Robert Stockton Williamson, who explored the Sierra mountain passes for a possible railroad route during the 1850s.

    Found in the central Sierra Nevada.

    Similar species: A pink-flowering species, **Dudley's clarkia** *(C. dudleyana),* often grows alongside *Clarkia williamsonii.* Its fan-shaped petals are streaked with white. It grows 20 to 30 inches tall and has 2- to 3-inch-long narrow leaves. It grows in the southern and central Sierra Nevada foothills. Another species, **rhomboid-leaf clarkia *(C. rhomboidea),*** has smaller, diamond-shaped petals with a long claw referred to by the species name. It grows 3 to 20 inches tall and has lavender or pink flowers about 1 inch long. You'll find it on dry slopes from Baja California to Washington and Montana.

Fireweed   *Epilobium angustifolium*

Fireweed readily comes into burned areas, sometimes covering acres with its tall stems and rose-colored flowers. It is not restricted to such a locale, however, also growing along roadsides, in fields, and in forest openings.

    Usually about 3 feet tall, fireweed may grow up to 6 feet in height if conditions are right. The brightly colored blossoms are borne on an elongated flower stalk. The flowers at the lower end bloom first, and it is possible to find unopened buds, fully opened flowers, and fruits all on the same plant. The 3-inch seedpods are four-sided. When mature, each pod splits into four linear segments, releasing seeds with tufts of white, silky hairs that act as parachutes, transferring the seeds over great distances. Fireweed is widely distributed in the Sierra, being found on both sides of the mountains and extending to timberline.

    Deer, elk, and domestic animals eat fireweed. The young shoots can also be used as a vegetable if cooked somewhat like asparagus. In addition, the leaves, either fresh or dried, can be used to make a hot tea.

    Found widely across North America, Europe, and Asia.

Farewell to Spring *Clarkia williamsonii*   **Fireweed** *Epilobium angustifolium*

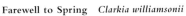

Farewell to Spring *Clarkia williamsonii*

California Fuchsia   *Epilobium canum*

By the latter part of August most of the wildflowers of the mountains, even those normally found at higher elevations, are spent. The leaves have shriveled and dried; stems have turned brown; fruiting pods or seeds have been blown by the wind, potentially to sprout the following spring when the snow has melted. The brightly colored California fuchsia is an exception. When most other mountain flowers have set seed, this wildflower may still be found blooming on dry slopes and ridges, sometimes clinging to a rocky granite crevice. The floral tube is scarlet or crimson and 1 to 2 inches long. The notched, floral lobes are shorter than the stamens, which protrude from the end of the tube.

These flowers attract hummingbirds, who stick their long beaks into the floral tube for nectar and the insects found in the tubes. For this reason, they are sometimes called hummingbird flower or hummingbird trumpet.

Found in much of California, into Oregon, Wyoming, and New Mexico. Also found in northern Mexico.

Rock Fringe   *Epilobium obcordatum*

Nestled amid the crevices of dry slopes and ridges near or even well above timberline, rock fringe creates small, green, leafy mats tucked between and over the rocky substrate. About 6 inches tall, it has bright red or rose flowers about 1 inch in diameter. Small, ovate leaves, opposite each other, are crowded onto the short stem. When in bloom, the brightly colored flowers appear to peek out from between the rocks and boulders. The name *rock fringe* perhaps results from the appearance of the flowers providing a fringe around the rocks. Look for it when hiking in the vicinity of Sonora Pass in the Toiyabe National Forest, Mount Whitney in the Inyo National Forest, and Castle Pass in the Tahoe National Forest.

Found from the Sierra Nevada north into eastern Oregon, central Idaho, and Nevada.

Evening Primrose   *Oenothera elata*

The flowers of evening primrose open in the evening and wither the next morning when hit by warm sunlight. Nonetheless, in the early hours of the day, they are quite conspicuous. They are large and showy, being 2 or 3 inches wide. When first open, they are pale yellow; however, they become an orange or reddish color as they wilt. The flowers are at the top of a stout, reddish stem, 3 to 6 feet tall. At most higher elevations, the plants grow only 3 to 4 feet tall.

Evening primrose is a biennial. This means that the primrose seed produces a rosette of basal leaves the first growing season. Only during the second year does the flowering stalk grow and produce the cluster of large yellow flowers familiar to so many mountain visitors. The plant is often branched and produces flowers throughout the entire summer. It grows in moist areas at moderate elevations.

Found widely in western North America and central America.

California Fuchsia *Epilobium canum*

Rock Fringe Evening Primrose newly opened flowers
Epilobium obcordatum *Oenothera elata*

FIGWORT FAMILY   Scrophulariaceae

The figworts comprise a worldwide family of some three thousand species, mostly herbaceous plants plus a few small shrubs. They generally have simple, alternate leaves. The floral parts are usually in fives, with the petals united to form a tubular, two-lipped basket. The figwort family contains many showy wildflowers, including paintbrushes, penstemons, and monkeyflowers, that cover meadows and openings throughout the mountain West. The common garden snapdragon is another member of this group, as is the medicinally important *Digitalis*.

PAINTBRUSHES   *Castilleja* species

The paintbrushes are among the most colorful wildflowers comprising our mountain flora. Most come in varying shades of red, pink, or sometimes yellow. There are some two hundred species of paintbrush, with more than thirty of these growing in California. Some can be very conspicuous, especially if they cover large areas. On the eastern slopes of the Sierra, they create glorious displays, contrasting with gray green sagebrush.

Though a paintbrush is easy to recognize, individual species are difficult to tell apart. This is because the most showy and conspicuous part of a paintbrush is not the floral petals but the ragged-edged bracts found below each flower and the floral sepals. These bracts are reminiscent of a paintbrush recently dipped into a paint bucket. The tubular corolla (united petals) is typically small and fairly inconspicuous, tucked down between the brightly colored bracts.

Most paintbrushes are at least partially parasitic on other plants' roots. Since they have green leaves, however, they also produce their own energy through photosynthesis.

Owl's Clover   *Castilleja exserta*

This delightful little wildflower grows 12 inches tall and is quite hairy, with leaves that are parted into threadlike segments. The purple or crimson flowers are about 1 inch long, the lower lip being white-tipped and spotted with yellow or purple. The bracts are purple or maroon. Primarily a springtime bloomer in California, owl's clover inhabits foothill areas and grassy meadows, where it may cover acres with its colorful blossoms. It flowers from April to June. Look for it as you drive along Foresta Road in Yosemite National Park or the Mineral King Road in Sequoia National Park.

Early settlers named this plant after the purple clover of Europe, which they felt it resembled. However, owl's clover is not related to the true clovers, which belong to the legume family. The Spanish name *escobita*, meaning "little broom," is perhaps more descriptive.

Found widely in California and into Arizona and northwestern Mexico.

Paintbrush on slopes of Round Top,
Eldorado National Forest

Owl's Clover   *Castilleja exserta*

Applegate Paintbrush   *Castilleja applegatei*

Applegate paintbrush inhabits a variety of plant communities, from sagebrush scrub to subalpine forests and alpine slopes, as well as the coastal mountains. It is a highly variable plant, with many subspecies. It grows 8 to 20 inches tall and has hairy, glandular foliage. The inch-long lanceolate leaves have crisp, wavy margins and are either entire or three-lobed. The floral calyx tips and bracts are scarlet or sometimes yellow.

Found in California and Baja California north into Oregon and Idaho, east into Nevada.

Meadow Paintbrush   *Castilleja lemmonii*

Meadow paintbrush is an erect or spreading plant noted for being hairy and glandular. It has several simple stems, 4 to 8 inches tall, and purple flowers and bracts. Its narrow leaves are 1 to 2 inches long, the upper ones usually divided. Found in moist meadows at upper elevations, it is common in Tuolumne Meadows in Yosemite National Park.

Found in the higher elevations of the Sierra Nevada and Cascade Range.

Indian Paintbrush   *Castilleja miniata*

This paintbrush is one of the most common and widely occurring paintbrushes of the Sierra. Its leaves are smooth and mostly entire, lanceolate in shape, and from 1 to 2 inches long. The erect, 2- to 3-foot-tall stems support large, red spikes. This paintbrush grows in moist areas from lower elevations up to timberline.

Found widely in California north to Alaska and also in the Rocky Mountains.

Chinese Houses   *Collinsia heterophylla*

Chinese houses is well named. The pagoda-like flower clusters resemble little houses, stacked on top of each other. Blooming in the springtime at lower elevations, Chinese houses grows 8 to 20 inches tall, with opposite, lance-shaped (sometimes toothed) leaves. The flowers are almost 1 inch long. The two-lipped corolla is pale lilac, pink, or purple, the upper lip being lighter than the lower. It is fairly common in shady areas in the foothills of the Sierra Nevada. In mid-May, you'll find it blooming in the dry roadsides near El Portal in the Stanislaus National Forest.

Found widely at lower elevations throughout California and also in northern Baja California.

Similar species: Innocence *(Collinsia tinctoria)* flowers are similarly shaped, but are pale green or white, with purple marks on the throat. The plant is somewhat glandular and is sometimes called sticky Chinese houses. It grows 8 to 24 inches tall with ovate or oblong leaves and is found up to 7,000 feet elevation in stony soils within mixed woodlands and coniferous forests. Look for it in the dry meadows around the Mather Ranger Station in Yosemite National Park.

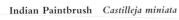

Applegate Paintbrush   *Castilleja applegatei*   **Meadow Paintbrush**   *Castilleja lemmonii*

Indian Paintbrush   *Castilleja miniata*   **Chinese Houses**   *Collinsia heterophylla*

Blue-Eyed Mary   *Collinsia torreyi*

Blue-eyed Mary or blue-lips, a widely distributed group of the *Collinsia* genus encountered in the Sierra, has two-lipped flowers with pale upper lips and deep blue lower lips. The flowers of most species are small, although their mass effect may be eye-catching. This species has rather large flowers, about a half-inch long. Inhabiting sandy flats and banks, it grows 2 to 8 inches high and has narrow, linear leaves and erect, branching stems.

Found in the higher mountains of California.

MONKEYFLOWERS   *Mimulus* species

Many species of Mimulus grow in the Sierra—some small, others large and showy. All have tubular, two-lipped flowers. Several of the more common ones are treated here.

Crimson Monkeyflower   *Mimulus cardinalis*

Also called scarlet monkeyflower, crimson monkeyflower is showy, with large, velvety, 2-inch-long flowers. It grows 2 to 4 feet tall and has hairy, sticky leaves that are oblong or ovate, somewhat clasping the stems. Three to five palmate veins spread through the leaves. These colorful flowers grow in wet areas, such as along stream banks, in moist meadows and seeps, or in bogs, along with other monkeyflowers, elephant's heads, and bog orchids.

This plant was introduced into European gardens by the intrepid botanist-explorer David Douglas from seeds he collected during his travels in California in 1830.

Found in California north into southeastern Oregon, east into the Great Basin and New Mexico.

Common Monkeyflower   *Mimulus guttatus*

Common monkeyflower is one of the more widespread monkeyflowers found in the western states. The 1-inch-long flowers are deep yellow, dotted with purple or brown in the throat. Common monkeyflower grows 1 to 3 feet tall and has leaves that are coarsely and irregularly toothed, with the upper ones stemless. This variable species grows mainly in rich, moist soils along streams and in meadows from sea level to timberline.

Found from California to Alaska east into the Rockies.

Similar species: Several other yellow-flowered monkeyflowers inhabit wet areas in the Sierra Nevada. *Mimulus tilingii* is similar but is usually smaller, growing 12 to 15 inches tall, with leaves that are often cool and slimy to the touch. Also, common monkeyflower usually has many blossoms on each plant; *M. tilingii* usually has only one to three flowers per stem. Growing close to the ground in wet places, **musk monkeyflower (*M. moschatus*)** has yellow flowers about 1 inch long. The entire plant typically has a musky odor. It barely grows 12 inches tall, and its leaves are covered with dense, white hairs. The dainty **primrose monkeyflower (*M. primuloides*)** has a single, yellow flower atop its slender 1- to 6-inch-tall stem. All the leaves, which are wedge-shaped, elliptic, or ovate, are basal. Sometimes the leaves have long, upright hairs that glisten like jewels when covered with dew.

Blue-Eyed Mary *Collinsia torreyi*

Crimson Monkeyflower *Mimulus cardinalis*

Musk Monkeyflower *Mimulus moschatus*
Inset: Primrose Monkeyflower *Mimulus primuloides*

Common Monkeyflower *Mimulus guttatus*

Lewis Monkeyflower
Mimulus lewisii

These pink blossoms, which resemble the cultivated snapdragon, grow along moist seeps and streams. The showy flowers are usually in pairs and are 1 to 2 inches long. They bloom from mid-June to early September. The tubular flower is two-lipped, with five spreading lobes, two turning up and three turning down. Since this species is so widespread, it varies greatly both in its foliage and in its flowers. For instance, even though the flowers are pale pink in the Sierra Nevada, they are deep rose in the Cascades. The common and specific names refer to the well-known explorer Captain Meriwether Lewis.

Found in the Sierra Nevada and Cascade Range, east into the northern Rockies.

Elephant's Head
Pedicularis groenlandica

The common name *elephant's head* is a direct reference to the oddly shaped reddish or purple flowers. The floral petals unite to form a two-lipped affair. The upper lip is strongly bent and extended, forming the elephant's "trunk." The lower lip is three-lobed, the two outer lobes bent back to form the elephant's flapping "ears." On close inspection it takes little imagination to see the flower stalk as a mass of elephant's heads, swaying in the mountain breeze. The showy spike of flowers, on a 6- to 24-inch-tall stem, most often grows in moist, open meadows, from mid-elevations to timberline. The leaves, mostly basal and up to 5 inches long, are lance-shaped but deeply dissected and resemble a dainty fernleaf. This distinctive plant usually blooms in July and August in the company of other moisture-loving wildflowers, such as monkeyflower, ranger's buttons, grass-of-Parnassus, and American bistort.

Found in the mountains of California north into Alaska, in the Rocky Mountains, and east across northern North America.

Similar species: Little elephant's head *(Pedicularis attolens)* also inhabits moist such sites as wet meadows, bogs, and seeps. The flower spikes in this species are covered with white hairs, and the plant itself is much smaller, growing between 6 and 16 inches tall. It, too, is found from mid-elevations to alpine areas, blooming from May through September.

Lousewort
Pedicularis semibarbata

This lowly plant dots the dry forest floor at middle and upper elevations. It has extensive underground stems, and its small, yellow flowers are often hidden beneath the deeply dissected, fernlike leaves. Lousewort's flowering stems grow only about 4 inches long, although its leaves may be as long as 6 inches. The yellow flowers have a hooded lip, giving it a lightly curved appearance.

Found in the mountains of California east into Nevada.

Similar species: Indian warrior *(Pedicularis densiflora)* resembles its common name. It has a dense cluster of crimson-red flowers, easily portraying the brightly colored headdress of an Indian brave. The finely dissected leaves are 4 to 7 inches long, and the flowering stalks are 4 to 20 inches tall. The plant is covered with soft, brown hairs, giving it a somewhat fuzzy appearance. It usually grows on dry, sunny slopes in the foothills and blooms in early spring.

Lewis Monkeyflower   Elephant's Head   *Pedicularis groenlandica*
    Mimulus lewisii   Inset: Little Elephant's Head   *Pedicularis attolens*

Lousewort   *Pedicularis semibarbata*

PENSTEMONS
Penstemon species

There are more than fifty species of penstemon in California, many of which grow in the Sierra. Although individuals are hard to tell apart, the group itself is easy to recognize. The flowers are a double-lipped basket, the upper lip consisting of two lobes, the lower lip of three. Penstemons have opposite leaves. Many spring from a woody base and could be called shrubby. The word penstemon comes from the Greek *pente,* or "five," and *stemon,* or "basket." Only four of the five stamens bear pollen; the fifth is sterile.

Davidson's Penstemon
Penstemon davidsonii

Growing on rocky, open slopes at timberline and above, this penstemon produces an exquisite display of tubular, purple flowers that are so large they cover and obscure the leaves. The ovate, evergreen leaves of this rock-hugging plant may only be a quarter-inch long, while the flowers are more than 1 inch long. Despite this small size (4 to 6 inches tall), Davidson's penstemon is sometimes considered a shrub because the stems grow from a woody base.

Davidson's penstemon exhibits many of the qualities required to survive at timberline. The plant is short, helping it avoid the brunt of the wind and fully utilize windbreaks, such as rocks, hollows, or boulders; it has evergreen leaves, allowing it to begin growth and photosynthesis as soon as the snow melts; its stems are closely grouped, allowing them to act as windbreaks and shelter for each other; and its flowers are a rich, dark color, aiding its absorption (rather than reflection) of sunshine.

This penstemon was named for Professor George Davidson, who collected specimens of the plant on Mount Conness north of Tioga Pass in 1890.

Found in the higher mountains of California north into Oregon.

Blue Penstemon
Penstemon laetus

Blue penstemon grows 1 to 2 feet tall and has pale blue or violet flowers an inch or more long. The gray green leaves are entire and linear to lanceolate. Blue penstemon is abundant in dry places at moderate elevations, especially in disturbed soil. Look for it along the Tioga Pass Road west of White Wolf in early July.

Found in mountainous areas of California north into Oregon.

Pride of the Mountain
Penstemon newberryi

No other wildflower can match the rosy red display of color put on by this penstemon, which anchors itself to crevices in rocky walls throughout the Sierra. Its most conspicuous display is probably along the granite roadcuts made by our cross-mountain highways. Inhabiting rocky, gravelly ground from moderate elevations to timberline, pride of the mountain resembles a small bush with numerous stems about 1 foot tall. The flowers bloom from June to early August. Look for it along the Heart Lake Trail in the Plumas National Forest or along the trail to Winnemucca Lake in the Moulkomne Wilderness of the Eldorado National Forest.

Found in the Sierra Nevada, the Cascades, and the mountains of northwestern California.

Davidson's Penstemon   *Penstemon davidsonii*

Blue Penstemon   *Penstemon laetus*

Pride of the Mountain   *Penstemon newberryi*

Bridge's Penstemon
Penstemon rostriflorus

This brightly colored penstemon rivals the color of scarlet gilia (see page 122). It grows 3 feet tall from a woody base and has lanceolate leaves that are 1 to 3 inches long. The inch-long floral tube is a perfect funnel for hummingbirds seeking nectar. Although found on the western slopes of the Sierra Nevada, it is more commonly seen on the eastern slopes, where it adds a splash of color to the sagebrush flats.

Found in the high mountains of southern and central California east into New Mexico and Colorado.

Meadow Penstemon
Penstemon rydbergii

This penstemon dots moist or drying meadows at middle and upper elevations, its deep purple flowers arranged in whorls around the upper portion of the stem. Meadow penstemon grows 8 to 24 inches tall. The tubular flowers, about a half-inch long, bloom from May through August, depending on elevation.

Found in the Sierra Nevada north to Oregon and east into Nevada.

Similar species: Sierra penstemon *(Penstemon heterodoxus)* grows in dry subalpine meadows and slopes and at timberline. Blooming in July and August, its deep purple flowers form whorls atop each stem. Its flower clusters are glandular, while those of meadow penstemon are smooth. It is also shorter, growing about 8 inches tall. Where both species occupy a single meadow, for instance at Tuolumne Meadows in Yosemite National Park, meadow penstemon grows in the lower, moist areas and Sierra penstemon inhabits the drier meadow margins.

FLAX FAMILY
Linaceae

The economically important flax family is rather small, consisting of about three hundred species. Linen thread, manufactured from a cultivated flax, is one of the most important vegetable fibers ever known. Western American Indians used flax fiber for strings and cords to make baskets, mats, fishnets, snowshoes, and other items.

Blue Flax
Linium lewisii

The bright flowers of the flax greet modern Sierra explorers, just as they did John C. Fremont, who wrote of the "common blue flowering flax," and Captain Meriwether Lewis, for whom it is named. The lovely blue flowers are about 1 inch across. They form a flat-topped cluster atop leafy stems that may grow as high as 30 inches, but 15 to 20 inches is more common. The leafy stems typically grow in clumps and have narrow, linear leaves about 1 inch long. Although common in lowland meadows, flax also grows in coniferous timber in the mountains and even on exposed ridgetops, such as those surrounding Sonora Pass and Donner Pass in the central Sierra. Blue flax is easily started in the garden from seed, which can be gathered near the end of the summer season and sown either in the fall or the following spring.

Found widely in western North America.

Bridge's Penstemon *Penstemon rostriflorus* **Meadow Penstemon** *Penstemon rydbergii*

Blue Flax *Linium lewisii* **Blue Flax** *Linium lewisii*

GENTIAN FAMILY Gentianaceae

The gentians are a worldwide group with about nine hundred species in the family. The family consists of annual and perennial herbs, with opposite or whorled leaves. The flowers are often showy, with floral parts in fours or fives. The corolla has united petals. Many gentians are cultivated for garden use.

Explorer's Gentian *Gentiana calycosa*

Gentians are commonly associated with mountain meadows, lending themselves to the beauty of the setting. This genus has erect herbs with showy flowers, the floral petals joined to make a somewhat funnel-shaped blossom. The four- or five-lobed flowers are green, blue, violet, or white.

Explorer's gentian has simple leafy stems with rounded inch-long leaves. Growing 5 to 15 inches tall, explorer's gentian has deep blue, funnel-shaped flowers, each about 1 inch long. A bluish membrane with several teeth connects the five floral lobes. The flower may be green dotted, adding to its beauty and charm.

Explorer's gentian prefers wet seeps and meadows at mid to upper elevations in red fir and subalpine forests. It can also be found in alpine areas at the edge of melting snowbanks. Sometimes it is very abundant, covering a slope or swale with its blue flowers. Look for it around Lake Tahoe near Fallen Leaf Lake and on the slopes above Emerald Bay.

Found from California north to British Columbia and Montana.

Similar species: Alpine gentian (*Gentiana newberryi*) is one of the more elusive Sierra wildflowers. Growing 1 to 3 inches tall, it has several stems that are prostrate or decumbent at the base. The inch-long floral tube displays a variation of color: white or pale blue or deep blue and dotted with green. Because of its small stature, you must look carefully among the sedges and grasses of the meadows where it grows. This gentian was named for John Newberry, who was a botanist on the survey trips exploring routes for a Pacific railway in the 1850s.

Sierra Fringed Gentian *Gentianopsis holopetala*

This common Sierra gentian grows as an annual or perennial. Its stems may be either erect or sprawling. The leaves are basal or occur near the base of the stems. The four-lobed flowers are dark blue, 1 to 2 inches long. Each flower is on a single stem, although several stems may make up a single plant. The lobes of the green calyx (the fused sepals) are typically dark-ribbed. The lobes of the corolla (fused petals) may have shallow, irregular teeth along the edge.

Sierra fringed gentian commonly dwells in damp meadows within the mixed conifer and red fir forests, as well as in alpine areas. It blooms from July to September. Look for it along the road over Sonora Pass.

Found in the Sierra Nevada north in the mountains to British Columbia and Montana.

Similar species: One-flowered or hiker's gentian (*Gentianopsis simplex*) has a single stem. The calyx lobes lack the dark rib found in *Gentianopsis holopetala*. The corolla lobes are fringed. It, too, grows in wet meadows and blooms from July to September.

Explorer's Gentian *Gentiana calycosa*   **Sierra Fringed Gentian** *Gentianopsis holopetala*

Monument Plant   *Swertia radiata*

Also called green gentian, this robust plant has elliptic leaves clustered at the base of the stem and a plume of closely packed flowers. It grows 3 to 6 feet tall and has flat, star-shaped, greenish white flowers. Each flower is 1 to 2 inches wide and is found in the axils of the leaves, which are 4 to 10 inches long. The leaves are opposite each other or grouped in whorls.

Monument plant grows in grassy spots and meadows within the lodgepole pine or red fir forests, nearly up to timberline. Look for it at Kearsarge Pass and Sonora Pass.

Found in the mountains from California and New Mexico north to Washington and South Dakota.

GERANIUM FAMILY   Geraniaceae

The geranium family contains less than three hundred species. Geraniums are annuals or perennials, with leaves that are palmately lobed or divided. The flowers are five-parted except for the number of stamens, which may be ten. The name comes from the Greek word for crane *(geranos)* because of the imagined resemblance of the long, fruit-bearing "beak" protruding from the center of the flower to a crane beak or bill. The geranium pistil, which has a long, pointed tip, releases its seed in a very peculiar way. When the fruit is ripe, each section of the seedpod (the "beak") separates elastically, curling from the base to the tip and releasing the seeds.

Richardson Geranium   *Geranium richardsonii*

Richardson geranium dwells in moist areas of the Sierra. Lake borders, wet meadows, or stream banks are logical spots to look for it. The five-petaled flowers are white or pale pink, with purple veins, and are about 1 inch in diameter. Growing at moderate to high elevations, it may be 1 to 3 feet tall and has large (up to 6 inches wide) basal leaves that are palmately parted five to seven times. The stem leaves are greatly reduced. Early in the season the leaves may look similar to those of the larkspur (see page 30) or monkshood (see page 26).

Found from southern California and northern Mexico north to British Columbia, and the Rocky Mountains.

Similar species: California geranium (*Geranium californicum*) grows at moderate and lower elevations in the central and southern Sierra Nevada. It is similar to Richardson geranium but is slightly smaller (8 to 24 inches tall), with rose red or occasionally white petals and darker veins.

Monument Plant   *Swertia radiata*   **Richardson Geranium**   *Geranium richardsonii*

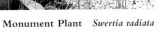

Monument Plant flowers   *Swertia radiata*

GOOSEBERRY FAMILY Grossulariaceae

The genus *Ribes* includes gooseberries and currants, which are shrubs with simple, alternate leaves. The outer flower parts unite to form a bell or saucer-shaped disk to which the petals are attached. Gooseberries and currants look similar, but one of the chief botanical differences is in the flowering stalks. In the currants the flowering stalks are jointed, so the berry breaks away. In the gooseberry, there is no joint, so the berry remains attached. Currant flowers are borne in clusters, while those of gooseberry are solitary or in pairs. In addition, the stems and often the berries of most gooseberries are armed with spines or prickles, while those of currants are not.

Wax Currant *Ribes cereum*

Wax currant, also called squaw currant, is a 3- to 5-foot-tall shrub with irregularly lobed, round leaves. The leaves are slightly sticky to the touch and have a spicy odor. The specific name *cereum* is derived from the Latin meaning "waxy glands" and refers to the leaves. The hanging, tube-shaped flowers are pink, pale green, or even white, with tips of the lobes turned backward. The berries are bright red, about a quarter-inch in diameter, and fall from the stalk when ripe in mid- or late summer.

Wax currant grows in forest edges, rocky slopes, and dry openings at mid-elevations.

Found from the southern Sierra Nevada and Arizona north to British Columbia.

Mountain Gooseberry *Ribes montigenum*

This small shrub grows in the partial shade of lodgepole and whitebark pine near timberline. A densely branched, scraggly shrub, it reaches 1 or 2 feet tall and has alternate leaves with five deeply cut lobes. The small, reddish brown or rust-colored flowers, about an eighth-inch long, are clustered inconspicuously beneath the leaves along the spiny stems. The orange berries that follow are covered with soft, edible bristles.

Found in the Sierra Nevada north to British Columbia and also in the Rocky Mountains.

Sierra Gooseberry *Ribes roezlii*

Sierra gooseberry is the most common gooseberry of the Sierra. It is a stout shrub, 2 to 4 feet tall, with spiny branches. The round leaves are about 1 inch wide and are cleft into three- to five-toothed lobes. The flowers have purplish or rose sepals and white petals. The berries, covered with long spines, are green in the early part of the summer, later turning red or purple. The flowers bloom in May and June.

Sierra gooseberry grows on dry, open slopes at moderate elevations or in the partial shade of red fir and ponderosa pine.

Found in the Sierra Nevada and Klamath Mountains.

Wax Currant   *Ribes cereum*
Inset: Wax Currant fruit   *Ribes cereum*

Sierra Gooseberry   *Ribes roezlii*

Mountain Gooseberry   *Ribes montigenum*

Sticky Currant
Ribes viscosissimum

Also called hairy currant, this is a bushy, spineless shrub with reddish bark that shreds easily. The leaves, young shoots, and berries are usually glandular—if you press a leaf between two fingers, it will cling to your skin. This trait is reflected in the name *viscosissimum*, a Latin word meaning "very sticky." The flowers are pink, dull green, or white. The alternate leaves are 2 to 3 inches wide and shallowly three-lobed with scalloped edges. The black, seedy berries ripen in August or September, and, although they have very little pulp, are eaten by birds, bears, and small rodents.

Sticky currant grows at middle to upper elevations beneath lodgepole and ponderosa pine, as well as in forest openings.

Found widely in the mountains of the western states.

HEATH FAMILY
Ericaceae

The heath family is a large group (with some three thousand species world-wide) of shrubs or small trees with mostly evergreen or leathery leaves. The stems or tree trunks commonly have shredding bark. Heath flowers are usually showy and are bell-shaped or urn-shaped.

MANZANITA
Arctostaphylos species

The manzanitas are an extremely important genus, found almost exclusively in the arid belts of California and southern Oregon, typically on dry slopes and hillsides, and usually in full sunlight. Manzanitas thrive on poor, stony soil and are well known for their ability to grow in burned areas. Many species sprout from unburned root crowns. Manzanitas are easily recognized by the distinctive character of their stems, leaves, flowers, and fruits. The stems and branches of the Sierran species are all rigid and usually crooked, with a smooth, shiny, dark red or reddish brown bark that peels off in thin strips. The leathery leaves are rarely toothed or notched. The small, pinkish or white, urn-shaped flowers form nodding clusters at the ends of the branches. Manzanitas are one of the earliest flowering shrubs in the Sierra foothills. The fruits, especially those of the larger species, resemble miniature apples—the name *manzanita* in Spanish means "little apple." Many California Indians made a cider from these fruits.

Pinemat Manzanita
Arctostaphylos nevadensis

Pinemat manzanita is a sprawling shrub, growing only 6 to 18 inches tall. It forms dense carpets on the floor of open forests, trailing over rocks and debris. The leaves, slightly over 1 inch in length, are elliptic. The flowers, a quarter-inch long, are white, sometimes with a pink tinge, especially as they begin to fade. Pinemat manzanita blooms in higher elevation ponderosa and lodgepole pine forests. It is common in the Gold Lake area of the Plumas National Forest.

Found throughout the Sierra Nevada and north through the Cascade Range.

Sticky Currant *Ribes viscosissimum*

Pinemat Manzanita *Arctostaphylos nevadensis*

Greenleaf Manzanita   *Arctostaphylos patula*

Greenleaf manzanita is one of the most widely spread and best known of the manzanita shrubs. It grows 3 to 8 feet tall and has quarter-inch-long drooping pink flowers that bloom from May to June. The leathery leaves are ovate or rounded, from 1 to 2 inches long, and bright green, in contrast to the dull green or whitish leaves of some species.

Greenleaf manzanita is a typical understory shrub in open ponderosa pine woodlands and is common at middle elevations throughout the Sierra Nevada.

Found widely in the mountains of the Pacific states north into Montana and Washington and also in the Rocky Mountains.

Similar species: Common manzanita *(Arctostaphylos manzanita)* grows at lower elevations and is an erect shrub, growing 6 to 12 feet tall (although taller specimens have been reported). The thick, elliptic or oblong leaves are bright green and about 1 inch long. The drooping flower clusters are pale pink or white. It most commonly inhabits the western slopes of the Sierra Nevada. Several other species are also found in the Sierra foothills. **White-leaf manzanita** *(A. viscida)* grows 4 to 12 feet tall and has whitish twigs and smooth, pale or gray green ovate to elliptic leaves. Its pink to white flowers form open clusters. The fruits have sticky surfaces. **Indian manzanita** *(A. mewukka)* grows 3 to 8 feet tall, has elliptical, grayish green leaves, white flowers, and smooth fruits.

White Heather   *Cassiope mertensiana*

Found in rocky banks and crevices near timberline, white heather, also called cassiope, greets those who sojourn in the high country. Its bell-shaped flowers are white (sometimes pale pink) and have five reflexed lobes. The leaves are pressed flat in tiers against the stems, forming overlapping scales. Like the red heather and many other alpine plants, white heather is a plant of low stature, the stems being only 4 to 12 inches tall. Instead of being erect, the white flowers nod from the tips of the creeping stems.

John Muir referred frequently to cassiope, leading many to believe it was his favorite alpine flower. He carefully described cassiope as bringing life to otherwise desolate and rocky mountain slopes: "Her blossoms . . . so beautiful as to thrill every fiber of one's being." Cassiope is not rare, but nonetheless, it is a delight to find. It grows in both alpine and subalpine areas and may form massive colonies that spread across the ground. It commonly grows alongside red heather (see page 70).

Found in the Sierra Nevada north to Montana and Alaska.

Greenleaf Manzanita *Arctostaphylos patula*   **White Heather** *Cassiope mertensiana*

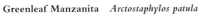

White Heather *Cassiope mertensiana*

Prince's Pine
Chimaphila umbellata

Also called pipsissewa or wintergreen, this shade-loving plant prefers cool, coniferous forests. Prince's pine is a shrubby little plant that spreads from underground rootstocks. It grows 4 to 8 inches tall, with shiny, loosely whorled leathery leaves. The leaves are somewhat lance-shaped, about 3 inches long, and toothed along the edges. Three to ten, pink, waxy-petaled flowers cluster at the top of the stems and almost appear to be upside down. The petals form an umbrella above the stamens and pistil, which hang underneath.

The genus name *Chimaphila* comes from the Greek for "winter-loving" and probably refers to the evergreen leaves, which retain their color throughout the winter.

Found widely in northern and western North America and also in northern Europe and Asia.

Similar species: Little prince's pine *(Chimaphila menziesii)* is a smaller plant, grows 3 to 6 inches tall, and has fewer flowers and leaves. Each flowering stalk has one to three flowers. The leaves are 1 to 2 inches long and are oblanceolate—meaning the lance-shaped leaves are wider at the outer end than at the base.

Alpine Laurel
Kalmia polifolia

The *Kalmia* genus is a small group of plants, with only a few species in North America. While alpine laurel is generally small and of low stature, one eastern *Kalmia* species is a small tree. Alpine laurel is a low, evergreen shrub, usually only 4 to 12 inches high. It has pink, saucer-shaped flowers composed of five spreading floral lobes and ten stamens. The slender, branched stems have sessile inch-long leaves with their edges rolled under, making them seem quite narrow.

Alpine laurel is fairly common in moist, boggy sites at higher elevations, where its pink flowers seem to dance in the ever present breeze.

Found widely in the mountains and coastal sections of western North America.

Labrador Tea
Ledum glandulosum

Nestled along rocky stream banks, usually in the partial shade of lodgepole pine, Labrador tea is found throughout the Sierra. If you hike along the Tuolumne River or near Glen Aulin in Yosemite National Park in early July, you'll find many of these shrubs in bloom. Labrador tea grows 2 to 5 feet tall and has round-topped clusters of white flowers at the ends of its branches. The leathery, evergreen leaves are oval or oblong, about 2 inches long, and occur alternately along the stem. The leaves have smooth edges, and tiny glands dot their undersides. Often the leaves have a fragrant odor, particularly when crushed.

Found through much of western North America.

Alpine Laurel *Kalmia polifolia*

Prince's Pine *Chimaphila umbellata*   **Labrador Tea** *Ledum glandulosum*

One-Sided Wintergreen   *Orthilia secunda*

This little wintergreen, also called side-bells, huddles at the base of conifers in deeply shaded forests. Its name comes from the pale green or cream-colored flowers that all hang from or turn toward the same side of the stem. The ovate or elliptic leaves grow along the base of the stems. One-sided wintergreen is about 6 or 8 inches tall and is often overlooked because of its inconspicuous flowers and small size.

Found throughout North America and also in Europe and Asia.

Red Heather   *Phyllodoce breweri*

This is one of the most delightful alpine flowers in the Sierra Nevada. Not elusive or rare, it is easily found near timberline and on open rocky slopes at higher elevations. The pink, bowl-shaped flowers, about one-half inch long, appear soon after the snow melts. A woody plant, red heather never grows very tall. Its thin stems are 6 to 12 inches high and covered with short, narrow, evergreen leaves that circle the stems. The ten protruding stamens make the flowers even more dainty.

You will find red heather, called bryanthus by John Muir, in the acid soil around high-elevation lakes and marshy spots or clinging to moist, rocky surfaces. Most hikers in July and August will encounter this mat-forming plant in subalpine and timberline areas, often in the company of cassiope. However, it also grows as a ground cover in shady hemlock, lodgepole pine, and red fir forests.

Found in the high mountains of California.

Pinedrops   *Pterospora andromedea*

A tall, brown-stemmed plant, pinedrops inhabits the floor of pine forests. Growing 1 to 3 feet tall, this plant consists of one or more stems with hanging, bell-shaped flowers on the upper portion of the stalk. Pinedrops has no green parts. The leaves have been reduced to small, brown scales along the stem. When the flowering stems first emerge, they are a rose red; after they have matured, the whole stem and floral remains turn brown and are conspicuous until the following spring, when new stems sprout. The stalks are sometimes gathered in late summer or fall and dried for floral decorations.

The roots of this plant, like those of snow plant (see page 74) are closely associated with the fungi that decay dead organic material. The fungi reduce the decaying matter, after which the roots of pinedrops absorb it. This association with fungi has allowed pinedrops to utilize a type of nutrition not used by green or chlorophyll-bearing members of the plant community.

Found widely in western and northern North America.

One-Sided Wintergreen   *Orthilia secunda*

Red Heather   *Phyllodoce breweri*

Pinedrops   *Pterospora andromedea*

Inset: Pinedrops after flowers mature
Pterospora andromedea

White-Veined Pyrola
Pyrola picta

Several species of pyrola or wintergreen inhabit the Sierra Nevada. They vary from a few inches to a foot or so in height. The cup-shaped flowers are arranged linearly along the stems and usually hang downward. In most cases, the leaves are basal, evergreen, and leathery in texture.

White-veined pyrola, also known as shinleaf, is easily recognized by its distinctive basal leaves, which are 1 to 3 inches long and a rich, dark green. The leaf veins are marked by white. The flowers are cream- or pale green and are found at the upper part of the 4- to 12-inch stems. Look for this little pyrola blooming along forested trails and in shady spots from June to August. It is fairly common on the floor of ponderosa pine forests.

Found in the mountains of southern California and New Mexico north to Alaska and also in the Rocky Mountains.

Similar species: Pink pyrola *(Pyrola asarifolia)* grows from a long, creeping rootstock. It has broad, rounded, leathery leaves 2 to 3 inches long. The leafless stems are 8 to 16 inches tall and bear five to twenty pink or red flowers. Found in moist, shaded areas at middle and lower elevations, this pyrola ranges from the Pacific states to the Atlantic.

Western Azalea
Rhododendron occidentale

A spectacular shrub when blooming at mid-elevations in June and July, western azalea prefers the shade of mixed conifer forests. It grows particularly well along stream banks and in moist or sheltered woodlands, where it may form dense thickets. Growing 2 to 14 feet tall, it is quickly recognized by its fragrant, 1- to 2-inch-long funnel-shaped flowers at the tips of the branches. The flowers are pink or white, with a large yellow blotch on the inner part of the upper lobe. Five stamens extend about 1 inch beyond the flower petals.

You will see the western azalea, a common Sierra shrub, along many of the roadways penetrating the western slopes of the mountains. It lines the roadsides between Yosemite Valley and Tuolumne Grove in Yosemite National Park.

Found in the coastal mountains and Sierra Nevada north into southern Oregon.

White-Veined Pyrola   *Pyrola picta*   Pink pyrola   *Pyrola asarifolia*

Western Azalea   *Rhododendron occidentale*

Snow Plant   *Sarcodes sanguinea*

This stout-stemmed plant attracts a great deal of attention because of its odd shape and brilliant red color. The fleshy stems are 1 to 2 inches thick and 6 to 12 inches tall. The scalelike leaves and bell-shaped flowers, like the stem, are bright red. Poking up through the duff and humus of the forest floor, particularly in the shade of towering red fir, snow plant resembles an emerging stalk of red asparagus. The common name is misleading. Although it blooms early in the summer, it does not normally push its way through snowbanks—unless covered with snow during an early summer snowstorm!

Snow plant has always intrigued Sierran visitors. John Muir noted more visitors admired snow plant than any other Sierran wildflower. However, it was evidently not his favorite plant. He described it in 1912 as a cold plant, standing alone and unmoved on the forest floor, even during wild mountain storms.

Like several other members of the heath family, snow plant lacks chlorophyll and derives its energy from dead plant material. Its roots do not even contact the soil in which it grows, but instead are enclosed by a casing of fungi, through which nutrients are transferred.

Found from southern California north to southern Oregon.

Sierra Bilberry   *Vaccinium caespitosum*

The Sierra bilberry, also called dwarf blueberry or huckleberry, is a tufted, sprawling shrub. It grows only a few inches tall and inhabits alpine and subalpine meadows above 7,000 feet, usually near a retreating snowbank. The small, oval leaves, barely an inch long, may cover rocky areas with a green carpet. The little pink flowers hide among the leaves, as do the bluish black berries, which ripen in August or September. It is in the late summer and early fall that these dainty plants are most conspicuous. Then the leaves turn a brilliant scarlet, painting the otherwise drab rocky slopes with color.

Finding ripe bilberries while hiking in the mountains is one of the rarest rewards of visiting the Sierra. Bilberries are fairly common in the high country, and the fruits are both sweet and tasty. However, because of their small size and the eager appetites of most small rodents, ripe berries are hard to find.

Found in the Sierra Nevada north to Alaska and Montana, across northern North America.

Similar species: The western blueberry (*Vaccinium occidentale*) is a low-growing shrub, usually found in moist meadows or along stream banks in subalpine areas or in wet spots in lodgepole pine and subalpine fir forests. The white or pink, urn-shaped flowers bloom in June or July. The blue-black fruits ripen in late August or September. They are about one-quarter inch in diameter and have a white bloom on their surfaces. This blueberry is found in the Sierra Nevada and Cascade Ranges of the Pacific states and also in the Rocky Mountains.

Snow Plant   *Sarcodes sanguinea*   **Western Blueberry**   *Vaccinium occidentale*

Sierra Bilberry   *Vaccinium caespitosum*

Red Huckleberry
Vaccinium parvifolium

This huckleberry has erect stems up to 12 feet tall and is distinguished by its bright red, rather than blue, berries. The stems are green and strongly angled. The thin, elliptic green leaves are not evergreen. Solitary pink or green flowers form in the leaf axils at the lower portion of the stems.

Red huckleberries are found in moist, wooded areas at lower elevations, typically growing from a rotted stump or log or other rich, decaying soil.

Found from the central Sierra Nevada and coastal mountains north to Alaska.

HONEYSUCKLE FAMILY
Caprifoliaceae

The honeysuckle family contains more than four hundred species of mostly shrubby plants, growing mainly in northern temperate regions. Honeysuckles, elderberries, snowberries, and viburnums all belong to this family.

Dwarf Honeysuckle
Lonicera conjugialis

Dwarf honeysuckle grows 2 or 3 feet tall and has thin, oval leaves 1 to 3 inches long. The small (about a quarter-inch long) paired flowers are dark red or purple and have protruding stamens. This attractive shrub grows on moist stream banks and in openings in conifer forests.

Found in northwestern California, the northern Sierra Nevada, and north into Washington.

Bearberry Honeysuckle
Lonicera involucrata

Also known as bearberry, inkberry, and twinberry, this is a freely branching shrub with paired yellow flowers. Broad, hairy bracts cradle the flowers and later enlarge, turn red, and become more conspicuous as the ink-black berries form. The twigs and branches of this honeysuckle are also paired and carry 2- to 6-inch-long oval leaves. Bearberry honeysuckle is one of the best known and more common honeysuckles in the western United States. It grows 2 to 5 feet tall, although occasional bushes 10 feet or more tall are encountered.

Bearberry honeysuckle adorns shady stream banks and moist glens at lower elevations in the Sierra Nevada and blooms in the early summer.

Found in coastal areas and mountains from Alaska to Mexico.

Red Huckleberry   *Vaccinium parvifolium*   Red Huckleberry fruits   *Vaccinium parvifolium*

Dwarf Honeysuckle   *Lonicera conjugialis*   Bearberry Honeysuckle   *Lonicera involucrata*

Blue Elderberry

Sambucus mexicana

Blue elderberry graces stream banks and moist flats or slopes, its flat-topped clusters of tiny flowers blooming through most of the summer. At lower elevations in the Sierra Nevada it blooms in early June, while in more sheltered spots at higher elevations (this elderberry grows up to about 10,000 feet) it may still be flowering in late August or September. The flower clusters are 2 to 6 inches across, occasionally even larger. These give way to blue berries. The opposite leaves are deep, dark green, pinately divided into five to nine leaflets. Blue elderberry is a many-branched shrub, 6 to 12 feet tall. Sometimes it grows to the size of a small tree of 20 to 25 feet. The tart, blue berries of this elderberry can be eaten raw, although most people prefer to make them into jam, jelly, pie, or wine.

The generic name comes from the Greek *sambuke,* a musical instrument that was made in part from elder wood. American Indians often referred to this bush as "the tree of music" because of the flutelike whistle they made from the pithy stems.

Found widely in the mountains and coastal areas of the Pacific states north into British Columbia and Alberta.

Red Elderberry

Sambucus racemosa

Red elderberry is a beautiful little shrub that grows between 6 and 20 feet tall along moist stream banks and in damp woodlands at middle elevations in the Sierra, but may only be a few feet tall along the trails leading into the high country. At upper elevations it may form low-growing thickets on rocky slopes. The plumes of creamy white flowers are dome-shaped and borne at the ends of the branches. The deep green, compound leaves have five to seven leaflets. It is, perhaps, the fruits of the red elderberry that attract the most attention. They are bright red and conspicuous when they appear at the end of summer.

Found through California north to Alaska and east into the central and southern Rocky Mountains.

Mountain Snowberry

Symphoricarpos rotundifolius

The hanging, bell-shaped flowers of this snowberry seem too dainty to cope with the alpine elements on the ridgetops and mountain passes where this bushy shrub resides. It thrives on dry, rocky slopes, and occasionally on the forest floor at lower elevations. About 3 to 5 feet tall, this shrub has dark green, inch-long leaves. The pink or whitish flowers are tucked between the leaves at the ends of the branches. The fruits that follow are white berries, hence the common name, snowberry.

Found in the Sierra Nevada north to British Columbia, east to Montana and Colorado.

Similar species: A trailing species found up to 8,000 feet elevation throughout most of the Sierra, **creeping snowberry (*Symphoricarpos mollis*)** has branches 1 to 3 feet long. It has a soft, hairy covering on the twigs, and the round leaves may have irregular lobes on them. Found in shady woods and other damp places, this plant has bell-shaped flowers that are bright pink, about a quarter-inch long.

Blue Elderberry *Sambucus mexicana*
Inset: Blue Elderberry fruit *Sambucus mexicana*

Red Elderberry *Sambucus racemosa*   Mountain Snowberry
Inset: Red Elderberry fruit *Sambucus racemosa* *Symphoricarpos rotundifolius*

Iris Family   Iridaceae

The iris family grows throughout the world and contains about fifteen hundred species. Many are cultivated, including the garden iris, crocus, and gladiolus. Identify the family by mostly basal leaves and showy flowers with three petal-like sepals, three petals, three stamens, and a three-parted pistil.

Western Blue Flag   *Iris missouriensis*

A patch of this pale blue iris adds beauty to any mountain meadow. Growing in small clumps, it is abundant in moist areas up to timberline throughout the Sierra. You'll find a lush display of it around North Lake in the Inyo National Forest and at Leavett Meadows in the Toiyabe National Forest. The large, showy, blue flowers are 2 to 3 inches across and appear on stems 8 to 30 inches tall. The broad, flat leaves grow about the same height. This flower blooms from May through August, depending on elevation, and its leaves stay green until after the flowers bloom. Then, if the meadow has begun to dry out, the plant also dries, leaving the three-parted seedpod in place of the flower.

Found widely in western North America.

Similar species: A smaller, less robust iris occurs in dry pine forests at lower elevations on the western slopes of the Sierra. **Hartweg's iris *(Iris hartwegii)*** rarely exceeds 12 inches in height and has narrow, linear leaves. Its flowers range in color from lavender to pale yellow or cream to a rich golden yellow. The golden yellow form is especially conspicuous around Pinecrest Lake in the Stanislaus National Forest.

Blue-Eyed Grass   *Sisyrinchium bellum*

This small wildflower of lush openings is indeed well named. The narrow, grasslike leaves barely look different from those of the surrounding grasses and sedges. The purple flowers appear as tiny eyes peering upward. Growing 6 to 24 inches tall from a cluster of fibrous roots, blue-eyed grass blooms throughout the summer. The stalked flowers protrude from a pair of sheathing bracts and are yellow at the base. A wide-ranging plant, blue-eyed grass is extremely variable and is often divided into several subspecies.

Blue-eyed grass is fairly common in moist forest openings, meadows, and grassy spots. Look for it around Soda Springs in Yosemite National Park.

Found in California and Oregon.

Similar species: Elmer's blue-eyed grass *(Sisyrinchium elmeri)* is a yellow-flowered species found in marshy places in the Sierra Nevada, the San Bernardino Mountains, and the Trinity Mountains. It is a small, tufted plant 6 to 8 inches tall. Look for it in Butterfly Valley in the Plumas National Forest.

Western Blue Flag *Iris missouriensis*   **Blue-Eyed Grass** *Sisyrinchium bellum*

Legume Family   Fabaceae

The legume family, also known as the pea family, is a large, cosmopolitan group of plants with some eighteen thousand species in the world. It contains herbs, shrubs, trees, and vines. Generally, the alternate leaves are compound, consisting of few to many leaflets. The flower parts are usually in fives and are often quite showy. The five petals of the flowers are arranged in two "lips." The upper petal is called the banner, while the lower two petals are united to form a keel. The remaining side petals are usually called wings. This basic arrangement describes all the flowers of this family. The common name *legume* refers to the fruits, which are usually a narrow pod.

This economically important group of plants contains species that are used for food or medicine, as well as many common garden plants, including the pea, peanut, lentil, alfalfa, clover, licorice, senna, sweet pea, and locust.

Redbud   *Cercis occidentalis*

Any traveler in the Sierra foothills between February and April will probably encounter a shrub covered with small pink, deep rose, or even purple flowers. You might look for it if you go to Ash Mountain in Sequoia National Park. This is redbud, a shrub that usually grows from 10 to 20 feet tall. The small flowers appear before the leaves, which are 2 to 3 inches long and nearly a perfect heart shape. When the leaves first open, they are a coppery color; later they become shiny green. The one-half-inch-long flowers grow in clusters along the stems and are later replaced by oblong pods that are dull red when mature. The pods remain on the tree into the following winter.

Found from the Sierra Nevada of California north into the Klamath Mountains, east to Utah and Texas.

Meadow Lotus   *Lotus oblongifolius*

Also called deer vetch, this colorful component of woodland edges and moist areas is recognized by its yellow flowers, adorned with a white keel. The keel is a common feature of the flowers of this family. Members of the genus *Lotus* have pinnately compound leaves, composed of smooth-edged (or entire) leaflets and pealike flowers. Growing 10 to 20 inches tall, this lotus has leaves with seven to eleven narrow or linear leaflets. The yellow and white flowers appear in clusters of one to five from May to August. The inch-long pods are shiny and black.

Meadow lotus grows on the floor of open pine forests, in moist meadows, and along river or stream banks at mid-elevations.

Found throughout the Sierra Nevada and in the Coast Range.

Similar species: The closely related **broad-leaved lotus (*Lotus crassifolius*)** grows in drier areas. It has yellow flowers marked with red that bloom from May through August on 2- to 3-foot-tall plants. The conspicuous pods may be 2 inches long and are green at first, turning a light brown or reddish color as they mature. The gray green leaves have nine to fifteen thick, oblong leaflets. This lotus, too, grows at middle elevations.

Redbud   *Cercis occidentalis*

Meadow Lotus   *Lotus oblongifolius*

LUPINE
Lupinus species

Lupines are a well-known group of western plants. Although individual species may be difficult to distinguish, the group itself is easily recognized by the palmately compound leaf (the leaflets originate from a common point, like the fingers of a hand) and the pea-shaped flowers. Lupines have alternate, usually long-stemmed leaves that may be covered with silky hairs. The number of fingerlike leaflets comprising the leaves varies between species, ranging from as few as four to as many as seventeen. The flowers are usually blue, but in some species are yellow, white, or even red. Only a few of the more common lupines are treated here.

Brewer's Lupine
Lupinus breweri

Brewer's lupine is a leafy, matted, often prostrate, plant. It has woody stems rarely exceeding 6 to 8 inches tall. The seven to ten leaflets of each leaf are about a half-inch long and covered by white, silky hairs. The flowers, less than a quarter-inch long, are blue or violet with a yellow or white center. Brewer's lupine is common in dry openings and clearings at moderate to higher elevations. Look for it along roads passing through the mountains.

Found from the southern Sierra Nevada north through the mountains to Washington.

Similar species: A similar-appearing plant on dry alpine ridges and slopes, **dwarf lupine (*Lupinus lepidus*)** forms low, woody tufts. Its leaflets are more acute or pointed than those of *L. breweri*. The mostly basal leaves have five to six lance-shaped leaflets, which are covered with flattened hairs. It is found from the Sierra Nevada north to British Columbia and also in the northern Rocky Mountains.

Broad-Leaved Lupine
Lupinus latifolius

This common lupine of mid-elevation open conifer forests grows 2 to 3 feet tall and resembles a small shrub. As the plant grows and matures during the summer, the lower leaves may dry by the time the flowers appear. The flowers bloom from April through July and are blue, purple, or sometimes pink. The leaves are composed of five to eleven leaflets that are somewhat hairy on the lower sides.

Found from Baja California and Arizona north to British Columbia.

Large-Leaved Lupine
Lupinus polyphyllus

This showy lupine is locally common and fairly robust, growing 2 to 3 feet tall. The large leaves are composed of ten to seventeen smooth-surfaced leaflets, and the flowers form pyramid-shaped clusters at the tips of the flowering stems. The flowers are pale blue or violet, sometimes with a reddish tinge. Look for large-leaved lupine in wet, boggy places or on the edges of wet meadows at middle elevations in the Sierra Nevada.

Found from California north to British Columbia.

Brewer's Lupine   *Lupinus breweri*

Broad-Leaved Lupine   *Lupinus latifolius*   Large-Leaved Lupine   *Lupinus polyphyllus*

Harlequin Lupine
Lupinus stiversii

Harlequin lupine is a freely branching annual that grows 4 to 20 inches tall. Its common name refers to its coloration—the upper petal is bright yellow, while the wings are pink or purple and the keel is white. These flowers are much larger than the other Sierran species covered in this book, being almost 1 inch long. The hairy leaflets are also about 1 inch long. Harlequin lupine grows in sandy and gravelly places in the foothills and ponderosa pine forests of middle elevations. It blooms from May to July.

Found from the southern Sierra Nevada north through Washington.

LILY FAMILY
Liliaceae

This large and important family of some four thousand species contains herbs, shrubs, a few trees, and some vines. Its members have leaves that are typically basal or alternate on the stem and that often wither early, before the flower finishes blooming. The petals and sepals may be similar or different, but are in threes. There are six stamens and a three-parted pistil. The family is rich in valuable plants and includes such species as the tulip, tiger lily, hyacinth, day lily, asparagus, and onion.

Sierra Onion
Allium campanulatum

This wild onion is one of several species found in the Sierra Nevada. Growing from 2 to 12 inches tall, Sierra onion is common and widespread, flourishing on dry road shoulders, banks, and gravelly slopes, and often presenting showy displays. It has two or three linear leaves, about the same length as the flowering stem. The cluster of rose or pink flowers has two small, leaflike bracts beneath it. There are from fifteen to forty of these flowers, each about one-third inch long and quite delicate in appearance.

Found widely in California and also in Nevada.

Similar species: A very similar species, *A. bisceptrum,* grows mainly on the eastern slopes of the Sierra. It also has rose-colored flowers. An easy way to tell the difference is to look at the leaves. Those of *A. campanulatum* are already withering when it blooms, while the leaves of *A. bisceptrum* remain green.

Harlequin Lupine *Lupinus stiversii*   **Sierra Onion** *Allium campanulatum*

Swamp Onion   *Allium validum*

This common and conspicuous onion grows in wet places throughout the Sierra Nevada. It lines shaded streams or grows in open marshes at middle and upper elevations. Its prevalence is attested to by place names such as Onion Valley in the Inyo National Forest, Onion Valley in the Stanislaus National Forest, and Onion Meadow in the Sequoia National Forest. A robust plant, swamp onion grows tall enough to let its cluster of rose red flowers stand above the surrounding rushes and sedges. The flattened flowering stems grow 1 to 3 feet tall and have grasslike leaves up to 2 feet long. These leaves emit an unquestionable onion odor (the specific name, *validum,* means "strong").

Take a small nip of a leaf and you will taste the strong flavor. Western pioneers used these leaves and the bulb as seasoning in stews, soups, and other dishes. You'll find plenty of swamp onion not only at Onion Valley but other places, such as around North Lake in the Inyo National Forest, in the wet areas of Tioga Pass, along the trails of the Desolation Wilderness of the Eldorado National Forest, and beside Sagehen Creek in the Tahoe National Forest.

Found widely in California north to British Columbia and east into Idaho and Nevada.

Harvest Brodiaea   *Brodiaea elegans*

Brodiaeas are showy herbaceous plants growing from a corm (a short, thick underground stem). They have basal leaves and flowers in umbels. The flowers usually stand erect, and the floral parts are fused to form a funnel-shaped or narrowly bell-shaped blossom. Harvest brodiaea is unusually showy, standing 4 to 16 inches tall. It has narrow leaves of about the same length that dry up by the time the dark blue flowers appear in late spring. Harvest brodiaea is distinguished by its three functional stamens, which alternate with three nonfunctional ones.

Harvest brodiaea is common on dry, grassy slopes, meadows, and woodlands at moderate to lower elevations in the Sierra.

Found in the Sierra Nevada north into southwest Oregon.

Swamp Onion *Allium validum*   **Harvest Brodiaea** *Brodiaea elegans*

Mariposa Lily
Calochortus leichtlinii

Mariposa lilies are among the most attractive flowers of the lily family. The genus is best known in the western United States, where various species are also known as sego lily, cat's ear, and star lily. *Mariposa* means "butterfly" in Spanish and refers to the beauty of the flowers. Found in open prairies, meadows, mountain hillsides, grassy forest floors, and alpine places, they grow from a bulb and have one or two narrow leaves at the base of the stem. The flowers somewhat resemble the cultivated tulip, with three petal-like sepals and three large, showy petals, each with a hairy gland near the base. The bulbs of most mariposa lilies are edible, and many western Indian tribes roasted them for food.

Calochortus leichtlinii not only is one of the more common of the Sierra mariposa lilies, but it also is one of the most beautiful. It has erect stems 8 to 16 inches tall and linear leaves. The bowl-shaped flowers are white, or, sometimes, a pale blue or pink. Each petal has a dark spot above the gland. This mariposa grows in open, stony places from middle elevations to timberline, and blooms from June to August.

Found in the upper elevations of the Sierra Nevada east into Nevada.

Similar species: A common foothill species is *Calochortus venustus,* which has large, showy bowl-shaped flowers that bloom in white, yellow, or purple. Each petal has a dark spot, often with a second pale spot of color above the first. It commonly grows along the dry, grassy road shoulders in the central and southern Sierra. *Calochortus bruneaunis* grows in dry, brushy places on the eastern slopes of the Sierra Nevada. The flowers are white, tinted with pale purple, with a crescent-shaped purple spot above the gland.

Star Tulip
Calochortus nudus

This low-growing plant, nestled amid fallen pine needles, catches one's eye. Growing barely 6 inches tall (although some specimens may be a bit taller), the star tulip has narrow, grasslike leaves and erect, white or purple flowers with rounded petals. The flowers are more open than those of the mariposa lilies, which have bowl-shaped flowers.

The name *Calochortus* comes from *kalos,* meaning "beautiful," and *chortos,* meaning "grass," and refers to the beautifully flowered plant with grasslike leaves. The species name *nudus* means "naked" and refers to the lack of hairs on the inside of the petals—most other species of *Calochortus* have a cluster of hairs at the base of the petal.

Found from the central Sierra Nevada north into southern Oregon.

Similar species: *Calochortus minimus,* which is more common in the central and southern Sierra, has nodding flowers with pointed petals.

Mariposa Lily *Calochortus leichtlinii*

Star Tulip *Calochortus nudus*

Common Camas
Camassia quamash

Camas has deep blue flowers composed of three sepals and three petals that are arranged symmetrically and look so alike the average observer assumes that the flower has six petals. It grows 8 to 14 inches tall with a leafless flowering stem. The basal leaves are linear.

Found in marshy spots, stream sides, and subalpine meadows, camas can cover a meadow or swale with its blue blossoms, looking much like a lake reflecting blue sky. Camas was one of the most important of all native plants for American Indians. Various Indian families cherished and held the camas .fields, guarding the coveted bulbs from their rivals. After the seeds were ripe, they dug the bulbs and baked or roasted them for at least twenty-four hours. Many settlers also learned to use the camas bulbs and even made pies from them. Care was always taken when digging camas, however, because the bulbs look like those of the white-flowered death camas (see page 100). Even Native Americans were known to have been poisoned from mistaking the death camas for the edible camas.

Found from California north into Canada and east into the central Rocky Mountains.

Soap Plant
Chlorogalum pomeridianum

Soap plant is conspicuous wherever it grows. Its stems reach 2 to 10 feet tall and branch like a candelabra. A cluster of waxy leaves, 1 to 3 feet long and with wavy edges, is found at the base of the stems. The small white or pale purple flowers near the tip of the tall stem have green or purple veins, making them quite distinctive. The name *Chlorogalum* probably comes from the Greek *chloros,* "green," and *gala,* "milk or juice," and refers to the sap. The descriptive name *pomeridianum* means "afternoon" and refers to the flowers' habit of opening in the afternoon. Soap plant grows best on dry, sunny slopes and fields below 5,000 feet, and blooms from June through August.

Soap plant has been used for making glue, and soap, for poisoning fish, and for food. The soap plant bulb contains a slippery substance that Native Americans used as a glue to make brushes; they used the fibrous material forming the outer covering of the bulb for the bristles. When rubbed, the inner parts of the bulb lather into a soap. The Indians also used the lather to help them catch fish. After damming a small stream and creating a lather in the water, they caught the dazed fish that came to the surface. Many California Indian tribes cooked the bulb for food, too.

Found in California north into southern Oregon.

Blue Dicks
Dichelostemma capitatum

Blue dicks dots grassy slopes and openings, its deep blue or purple flowers waving in the springtime breeze on its thin stems. It grows between 12 and 24 inches tall and has leafless stems. The basal, grasslike leaves are dry and disappear early in the summer. The tubular flowers are about a half-inch long and bloom from March through May in the foothills.

Found widely in California north into Oregon, east into the central and southern Rocky Mountains.

Common Camas *Camassia quamash*

Blue Dicks *Dichelostemma capitatum*

Soap Plant *Chlorogalum pomeridianum*

Sierra Lily
Lilium kelleyanum

Its delicate orange flowers bobbing in the faintest breeze, the Sierra lily adorns stream banks and moist places. Looking very much like the cultivated lilies of our lowland gardens, Sierra lily is one of the larger wildflowers of the mountains and is usually found in the graceful company of elephant's head and bog orchid. Growing 2 to 6 feet tall and having oblong leaves in whorls near the upper portion of the stem, Sierra lily produces nodding orange flowers, distinguished by their recurved petals. They are mildly fragrant.

Found at mid-elevations in the central and southern Sierra Nevada.

Similar species: Leopard lily *(Lilium pardalinum)* grows 3 to 8 feet tall and forms large groups along stream banks and wet areas at lower elevations. The nodding, bell-shaped flowers are yellow or dark red and have petals 2 to 4 inches long. Like those of the Sierra lily, the flower petals are recurved. However, Sierra lily flowers are much smaller, usually less than 2 inches long.

Alpine Lily
Lilium parvum

Alpine lily, also called small leopard or tiger lily, is recognized by bell-shaped flowers that are erect or horizontal, not drooping or nodding (as in the leopard lily and Sierra lily). The flowers are rose, orange, or yellow, and have maroon spots. Alpine lily grows up to 6 feet tall from a horizontal bulb. The showy flowers are trumpet-shaped and 1 to 2 inches long. The two to six leaves form whorls on the stem. Preferring moist areas, it is especially common in partially shaded glens near the roadsides along Lake Tahoe.

Found in the northern and central Sierra Nevada.

Washington Lily
Lilium washingtonianum

Growing on the brushy hillsides of lower-elevation chaparral and in mid-elevation pine forests, the Washington lily closely resembles an Easter lily. The showy, fragrant blossoms are white, sometimes becoming pink or purple on maturing. The spreading flowers are near the upper portion of the stem, which may be 2 to 6 feet tall. The leaves form several whorls along the length of the stem. Though they reach their peak in July, the flowers will still be found in some areas in early August. Watch for them along the Feather River in the Plumas National Forest in early July.

The Washington lily is a good example of the problems inherent in using common names. In northern California it is known as the Shasta lily, while in the Oregon Cascades it goes by such names as Mount Hood lily or Santiam lily, depending on the local area.

Found in the Sierra Nevada north in the Cascade Range to the Columbia River.

Sierra Lily   *Lilium kelleyanum*

Alpine Lily   *Lilium parvum*   Washington Lily   *Lilium washingtonianum*

Bog Asphodel
Narthecium californicum

Bog asphodel is pleasant to encounter. It grows from creeping rhizomes that spread through the damp soil, resulting in many plants occupying any given area. The stems are 8 to 24 inches tall, and have mostly basal, linear leaves that hide amid the reeds and sedges of its soggy habitat. Although the individual flowers are small, they crowd onto the upper portion of the stem and make a showy display. The perianth has six petal-like parts, which are yellow or tinged with green. You'll find bog asphodel in the company of other plants that like their feet wet, such as the bog orchid, camas, and wild onion. Look for it in Butterfly Valley in the Plumas National Forest.

Found in the central and northern Sierra Nevada and northwestern California.

False Solomon's Seal
Smilacina racemosa

Recognize false Solomon's seal by its plume of small, white flowers at the end of an erect, unbranched stem. The erect stems grow 1 to 3 feet tall and have alternate oblong or ovate leaves. The flowers form a plume at the end of the stem and bloom from April through June, depending on elevation. They are followed by red berries. False Solomon's seal is fairly common in shady woodlands at moderate elevations.

Found in the mountains of California north to Alaska and east across North America.

Star-Flowered Solomon's Seal
Smilacina stellata

Star-flowered Solomon's seal is similar to false Solomon's seal but is a smaller plant, up to 24 inches tall. The stem has a zigzag appearance, with leaves that clasp the stem. The flowers also form a terminal cluster, but it is smaller and daintier. The berries are red. Often star-flowered Solomon's seal is hidden in the brush of moist swales or stream banks. At other times it is quite lush, with many stems emerging from the underground rhizome.

Found in California north to British Columbia and east across North America.

Tofieldia
Tofieldia glutinosa

Tofieldia grows 8 to 28 inches tall and has linear, grasslike leaves that are sticky to touch (*glutinosa* means "sticky"). The cream-colored flowers are borne in terminal clusters. Blending into the surrounding grasses and sedges, tofieldia is noticeable when bearing both its perky plume of flowers and its ruby-tinted fruits. Look for it in the company of death camas (which it closely resembles), bog orchid, gentian, and Labrador tea.

Found in the Sierra Nevada north to Alaska and western Canada.

Bog Asphodel   *Narthecium californicum*   **False Solomon's Seal**   *Smilacina racemosa*

Star-Flowered Solomon's Seal   Tofieldia
               Smilacina stellata   *Tofieldia glutinosa*

Hyacinth Brodiaea   *Triteleia hyacinthina*

Most of the wildflowers commonly called brodiaeas are blue or purple. This species, however, has white flowers. The erect stems grow 12 to 24 inches high and have grasslike, linear leaves. The flowers are in a terminal umbel. They are white, sometimes tinged with blue, and have dark veins. It grows at mid-elevations on grassy slopes or drying meadows.

   Found in California north into British Columbia and east into Idaho.

Ithuriel's Spear   *Triteleia laxa*

Also called *grass nut* and wally basket, this is a robust and fairly common wild-flower, with leafless stems up to 3 feet tall. Ithuriel's spear has pale blue or purple flowers in an open umbel at the top of the stem. The individual flowers are tubular and almost 1 inch long. They bloom from April through June and inhabit open, grassy places such as the Ash Mountain area of Sequoia National Park.

   The name *grass nut* refers to the small corm (short, thick, underground stem) that Indians prized for its nutty flavor.

   Found widely in the mountains of California into southwestern Oregon.

Golden Triteleia   *Triteleia montana*

Several of the common triteleias have golden or straw yellow flowers. This wildflower grows 2 to 10 inches tall and has an umbel of flowers that are particu-larly conspicuous when it covers a drying meadow or roadside in midsummer. Each flower is funnel-shaped and is striped with brown on its underside.

   Found in the northern and central Sierra Nevada.

Corn Lily   *Veratrum californicum*

Also called false hellebore, this tall, stout plant grows from 3 to 6 feet tall and has large, parallel-ribbed leaves. However, it is the plume of white flowers that is most conspicuous. The drooping blossoms appear in July and August through-out the Sierra Nevada. Corn lily usually grows in small clumps, a trait making it even more notable, poking its way through the ground in wet areas, basking in snow meltwater. It is plentiful in marshy spots, along stream banks, and in wet meadows. The common name refers to the general appearance of the plant, which resembles cultivated corn. Often, by late summer, when the blos-soms have long faded, the leaves become delicately laced after being nibbled and eaten by insects or shredded by hailstones.

   Corn lily has been reported as poisonous, with the roots and young shoots being considered the most toxic. As the plant grows and matures, however, it becomes less toxic and is usually considered harmless after a frost.

   Found widely in the western United States.

Hyacinth Brodiaea   *Triteleia hyacinthina*   Ithuriel's Spear   *Triteleia laxa*

Golden Triteleia   *Triteleia montana*   Corn Lily   *Veratrum californicum*

Joshua Tree
Yucca brevifolia

This conspicuous treelike member of the lily family grows up to 30 or 40 feet tall. It may be openly branched or grow as a main stalk. The flowers, clustered near the ends of the branches, are bell-shaped, 5 to 6 inches long, and pale green or cream in color. The petals feel somewhat leathery. The flowers bloom in early spring and are very fragrant. The fruits are the size of a large egg and drop to the ground when ripe.

Joshua trees grow in the southeastern Sierra Nevada, where they migrate up the canyon slopes and may be locally common.

Found in the deserts of southern California and into western Arizona and southwestern Utah.

Our Lord's Candle
Yucca whipplei

Also called chaparral yucca, this tall, conspicuous member of the lily family lines many roadways into the southern Sierra Nevada. It may grow 15 to 20 feet tall and has a dense cluster of sharp, needle-tipped linear leaves at the base of each stalk. The gray green leaves are 2 to 4 feet long. The clusters of leaves may dot the dry slopes of chaparral foothills, each plant growing for several years before sending up a flowering stalk that looks like a giant spear of asparagus as it emerges. The flowers are showy and bloom in plumes at the top of the stems. Once the plant has flowered, it dies; however, the stalk may remain upright for several years.

Native Americans used the fibers from yucca leaves to weave into a coarse cloth or twine. The seeds were gathered and used for food.

Found in the southern Sierra and southern California into Baja California.

Death Camas
Zigadenus venenosus

Growing from small, oblong bulbs, this plant is sometimes called white camas to distinguish it from the blue-flowered camas (see page 92). The 10- to 20-inch stems have plumes of white flowers near the tip and linear leaves, which are somewhat folded and are clustered at the base of the stem. The white or cream-colored flowers form a round-topped cluster at the end of the stems. Death camas grows at lower elevations on dry slopes and meadows and may also inhabit openings in ponderosa pine forests.

All parts of death camas are toxic. Cattle or sheep sometimes eat the plant early in the summer, when it is still succulent, and suffer from poisoning. By the latter part of the summer, death camas has usually dried and so is not very palatable.

Found widely in the western and central United States; also in British Columbia and Baja California.

Similar species: Death camas could be confused with the common blue-flowered camas, and they do sometimes grow together. Death camas is usually found in dry soil. However, this includes meadows that may be moist in the springtime but dry by the end of the summer, leading to possible confusion with the edible blue camas. Anyone gathering camas bulbs for food should always take care to identify them correctly.

Joshua Tree   *Yucca brevifolia*

Our Lord's Candle   *Yucca whipplei*   Death Camas   *Zigadenus venenosus*

LOASA FAMILY   Loasaceae

The loasa family consists of about two hundred species of annuals and perennials or shrubs. The plants are noted for their rough hairs, which may be almost needlelike in texture; some even sting. The flower parts are in fives, but with many stamens. Members of this family usually inhabit dry areas. A few showy species may be found in gardens.

Blazing Star   *Mentzelia lindleyi*

Dancing gaily in the sunshine, blazing star grows best in dry, open areas below 4,000 feet, where its butter-colored flowers add brightness to the drying grasses of foothill areas in late spring and early summer. This blazing star grows 6 to 24 inches high and has pinnately lobed leaves that are 2 to 6 inches long. The leaves have bristly white hairs that cling to anything they touch, giving rise to another common name, stickleaf. The leaves and stems feel like fine sandpaper. The five-petaled flowers are 2 to 3 inches across, and each petal has a small point on its tip.

Found widely in the coastal and mountainous areas of California.

Similar species: Another species of blazing star, **Mentzelia laevicaulis,** blooms later in the summer, usually from June through October, and is distinguished by its narrower, longer petals, which may be 2 to 3 inches long. It grows on both sides of the Sierra, ranging up to 8,500 feet elevation, and is most often encountered in dry places. It is particularly conspicuous in disturbed soil bordering roadways leading into the mountains. Found through most of the Sierra Nevada, it can grow to 3 or 4 feet tall but is usually much shorter.

MALLOW FAMILY   Malvaceae

The mallow family is well known because of the many ornamental plants, such as hibiscus and hollyhock, belonging to the group. The *Sidalcea* genus has more than twenty species, mostly in California and Oregon.

Smooth Sidalcea   *Sidalcea glaucescens*

This mallow, with its loosely arranged pink flowers, is a notable component of the plant community found on grassy slopes and dry, open meadows from the foothills nearly to timberline. Its smooth stems are 1 to 2 feet long and have leaves that are deeply lobed into five to seven narrow divisions. The pale flowers are about 1 inch across and appear from May to July in places such as Crane Flat in Yosemite National Park and the Pinecrest area of the Stanislaus National Forest.

Found from the southern Sierra Nevada to northern California and also in Nevada.

Similar species: Checkerbloom *(Sidalcea malvaeflora)* grows 1 to 2 feet tall and has flowers that are 1 to 2 inches wide. Its stems and petioles, however, are not smooth but have short, coarse hairs. Checkerbloom has two types of leaves, the lower ones being bluntly lobed and the upper ones being divided and toothed. Checkerbloom is widespread in the Pacific states and is quite variable.

Blazing Star *Mentzelia lindleyi*   **Smooth Sidalcea** *Sidalcea glaucescens*

Oregon Sidalcea
Sidalcea oregana

The mallows are some of the prettier components of wet meadows, especially since they bloom into August, when other meadow flowers have begun to fade. The flowers of this mallow are commonly closely clumped together at the tip of the stems, which are from 1 to 5 feet tall. The round leaves are 1 to 4 inches wide, the basal ones with five to seven shallow lobes and the upper stem leaves deeply divided into about seven narrow lobes. Oregon sidalcea is common throughout the Sierra and can be found in early August at Round Meadow in Sequoia National Park or in July at Hope Valley in the Toiyabe National Forest.

Found in the Sierra Nevada north into Oregon and Washington.

MILKWEED FAMILY
Asclepiadaceae

The milkweed family contains nearly three thousand species of plants that reside mainly in the tropics, subtropics, and southern Africa. They are annuals, perennials, shrubs, or vines with milky sap. The leaves are simple, usually opposite or whorled, and the flowers form branched clusters or are solitary. The flowers usually have five reflexed sepals, five spreading or reflexed petals, five stamens, and two ovaries. A few members of this family, for example butterflyweed, are planted as ornamentals.

Showy Milkweed
Asclepias speciosa

Several species of milkweed grace dry fields, roadsides, and other open areas of the Sierra Nevada and are characterized by their distinctive flower arrangement, which consists of five petals and five reflexed sepals, and milky sap. This milkweed has rosy or purple flowers in round, showy clusters toward the upper end of a 1- to 4-foot-tall stem. The specific name, meaning "showy" or "spectacular," refers to this mass of flowers. The gray green, oval or elliptic, woolly leaves are 3 to 6 inches long and sit opposite each other on the stem.

Found in the foothills and lower conifer forests on dry, open sites, often along roadsides. This milkweed grows from California north to British Columbia and central Canada and east to the Mississippi Valley.

Similar species: Purple milkweed (*Asclepias cordifolia*) grows up to 2 feet tall and has broad, heart-shaped, clasping leaves that are about 6 inches long. Its flowers are a dark reddish purple. **Narrow-leaf milkweed (*A. fascicularis*)** has extremely narrow leaves that are often folded along the midrib. The leaves are 1 to 5 inches long and about a quarter-inch wide. They are usually in whorls of three to six on a 1- to 3-foot-tall stem. The flowers are greenish white, sometimes tinged with purple. A particularly hairy plant, **Indian milkweed (*A. eriocarpa*)** is about the same size. It has creamy or purple-tinged flowers and 6-inch-long, oblong leaves that are either opposite or whorled.

Oregon Sidalcea *Sidalcea oregana*   **Showy Milkweed** *Asclepias speciosa*

MINT FAMILY
Lamiaceae

The mint family is generally distinguished by the fragrant aroma of its members. Another distinguishing trait is its four-angled stems. If you take the stems in your fingers, they will not roll, because they are not round. Mint leaves are generally opposite each other on the stems and can be simple or deeply lobed. The floral petals usually form a two-lipped tubular flower, which can be very showy. This is a worldwide family consisting of more than five thousand species. The group is known mainly for its volatile oils, which are used for medicines and flavorings. Well-known members of this family include rosemary, thyme, lavender, peppermint, and spearmint.

Giant Hyssop
Agastache urticifolia

The plumes of flowers adorning the giant hyssop, also known as horsemint, line the openings and roadways of Yosemite Valley in July or Sonora Pass in August. A fragrant plant, it grows up to 5 feet tall. Like other members of the mint family, the stems are square and the flowers two-lipped. The tubular flowers are white, rose, or purple. Two pairs of stamens protrude from the floral tube, like spectators in a box seat. The flowers are in thimble-shaped clusters that may be 4 inches long. The flowers bloom in midsummer; individual plants last only a few days.

Giant hyssop thrives in a wide variety of soils and exposures: dry, gravelly, moist, or sandy areas in meadows, brushlands, or open woodlands.

Found from southern California north to British Columbia and also in the Rocky Mountains.

MINTS
Monardella species

Also known as pennyroyal, this genus contains colorful and fragrant members of the Sierra Nevada wildflower community. The flowers are in bracted heads. If you take a few minutes to examine mint flowers carefully, you'll find a dainty, tubular basket with two lips, the upper erect and cleft into two lobes, the lower lip parted into three segments. Four stamens protrude from the basket.

Mustang Mint
Monardella lanceolata

Mustang mint grows at lower elevations. It is an erect annual growing 6 to 24 inches tall. The stems branch into several floral clusters. The linear leaves are 1 to 2 inches long. The floral heads are an inch across and composed of reddish or purple flowers. Mustang mint is abundant in dry areas at moderate and lower elevations.

Found from the Sierra Nevada south through southwestern California to Baja California.

Giant Hyssop *Agastache urticifolia*   **Mustang Mint** *Monardella lanceolata*

Mountain Pennyroyal   *Monardella odoratissima*

This colorful mint can be found widely in the Sierra Nevada and has several varieties and subspecies. It grows 9 to 18 inches tall, the entire plant
being slightly hairy. Its lance-shaped leaves are about 1 inch long. The flowers are pale lavender or white and form round-topped clusters at the tips of
the stems. Mountain pennyroyal grows in small clumps on dry slopes in
coniferous forests or on exposed ridges from moderate elevations into subalpine and alpine zones. You'll find it along the trail to Heart Lake in the
Inyo National Forest, in Tuolumne Meadows in Yosemite National Park,
and along the roadways over many Sierra Nevada mountain passes.

Pennyroyal makes excellent tea and is often gathered for that purpose.
The leaves can be used fresh or dried.

Found through the Sierra Nevada north into Oregon and also in the
Rocky Mountains.

Self-Heal   *Prunella vulgaris*

Self-heal inhabits moist, shaded areas or meadows. It grows 4 to 12 inches tall
and has opposite oblong or ovate leaves that are 1 to 3 inches long. The small
pink or purple flowers are two-lobed baskets that grow in dense terminal
spikes. The flowers are quite ornate—the lower lobe is three-parted, the upper
lobe forms a hood.

Self-heal grows in a wide range of habitats—in carefully manicured lawns
or hidden amid the grasses of wild meadows. The plant is able to adapt to a
wide variety of situations, as reflected in the name *vulgaris,* meaning "common." It grows from sea level to upper-elevation meadows. One good place to
look for it is in Quaking Aspen Meadow in the Sequoia National Forest.

The name *self-heal* comes from the plant's reported value as a remedy for a
variety of ailments, from chest pains to a sore throat. The genus name *prunella*
is derived from the name of a European plant used to treat chest pains.

Found widely across North America and also in Europe and Asia.

White Hedgenettle   *Stachys albens*

White hedgenettle is well named, because it is covered with soft, woolly, white
hairs. As the plant matures, the hairs become matted and cobwebby. Most
hedgenettles are rather rank, coarse plants, falling into disfavor for their resemblance to stinging nettles, which are in another family. White hedgenettle has
white or pinkish tubular flowers that are two-lipped, the upper lip erect and
the lower lip spreading. Although the individual flowers are small, they are
pretty and ornate. White hedgenettle grows 1 to 4 feet tall in moist woodlands
and meadows below 8,000 feet throughout the Sierra.

Found from the mountains of northern California to the southern Sierra
and also in the White Mountains.

Mountain Pennyroyal *Monardella odoratissima*

Self-Heal *Prunella vulgaris*   White Hedgenettle *Stachys albens*

MOCK ORANGE FAMILY   Philadelphaceae

The mock orange family contains about 130 species of small shrubs. The bark of these shrubs is usually shredding or peeling. The leaves are simple and opposite on the stem. The flowers are in showy clusters, which are either terminal or tucked into the axils of the branches.

Mock Orange   *Philadelphus lewisii*

Also called syringa, this plant is a widely distributed and very showy flowering shrub that grows on rocky slopes and grassy fields at lower elevations. Although not extremely common, it stands out because of its clusters of fragrant white flowers. Growing from 4 to 10 feet tall, it is a loosely branched shrub with 3-inch-long, opposite leaves. The beauty and sweet scent of this flowering shrub have made it a popular ornamental and earned it fame as the state flower of Idaho.

The species name honors Captain Meriwether Lewis of the Lewis and Clark Expedition, who collected the plant in 1806 along the Clark Fork River in Montana.

Mock orange might be confused with mountain dogwood (see page 40) or bitter cherry (see page 150), both of which are also shrubs with clusters of white flowers. However, mountain dogwood usually grows in moist areas, not dry, rocky slopes. Bitter cherry has white flowers in round-topped clusters, and its leaves are grouped together on short twigs instead of being opposite each other on the branches.

Found from the Sierra Nevada north into British Columbia and Montana.

MUSTARD FAMILY   Brassicaceae

Mustards comprise a large group. They are widespread and variable, with many plants of economic value. Cabbage, radish, cauliflower, turnip, and rutabaga are only a few of the more commonly known garden plants belonging to this versatile family. Still other mustards fall under the category of weeds, invading wastelands and farmland alike. As a group, mustards are identified by a watery juice, alternate leaves, and a diagnostic flower. There are always four sepals and four petals, which spread opposite each other to form a cross. One Latin name for the family is Cruciferae, meaning "cross." There are six stamens (rarely four or two), two of which are much shorter than the other four. All mustards are a variation of this general pattern.

Draba   *Draba lemmonii*

A compact crown of bright yellow flowers identifies this typical member of the alpine flora. It may be found in many of the high-elevation passes and basins—look for it among the rocky crevices of Humphreys Basin in the John Muir Wilderness in the Sierra National Forest or on the rocky slopes of Mount Dana. The dense cluster of stems rises only a few inches from the ground. The leaves, less than one-half inch wide and oblong with a narrow base, produce a dense cushion of foliage. The golden flowers are in a tight cluster and appear in July and August. A short, twisted pod bearing the seeds follows the fading of the flowers.

Many explorers and botanists collected plant specimens in the mountains of California during the late 1800s. John G. Lemmon visited Yosemite in 1878, having come to California several years earlier after being released from a Confederate prison when the Civil War ended. He became an avid plant collector, discovering this one on Mount Lyell in Yosemite National Park. Another plant named in honor of Lemmon is *Castilleja lemmonii* (page 48).

Found in the Sierra Nevada and also in the Wallowa Mountains of northeastern Oregon.

Mock Orange   *Philadelphus lewisii*

Draba   *Draba lemmonii*

Western Wallflower
Erysimum capitatum

Wallflowers add a dash of bright color to rocky bluffs and cliffs. Although the mustard family itself is large and variable, this genus is fairly distinctive, with its showy, round-topped cluster of flowers. Wallflower is a robust, coarse plant, frequently found in stony slopes and swales. The color of the flower varies widely. Most often a bright orange, it may also be yellow, burnt red, or maroon. At middle elevations it has somewhat hairy stems growing 1 to 3 feet tall with narrow leaves that are 3 to 6 inches long.

At higher elevations western wallflower is quite a bit smaller, growing only 4 or 5 inches tall. Then the brightly colored flowers are very conspicuous atop the short plants. On alpine slopes wallflower displays a characteristic that helps it adapt to the shorter growing season and long winter. Leaves from the previous year die back and protect the root crown, from which the next year's stem emerges.

Found widely in western North America.

Shieldleaf
Streptanthus tortuosus

Shieldleaf is an unusually pretty mustard that grows 8 to 36 inches tall. The purple or yellowish flowers are about one-half inch long, with slightly recurved sepals and twisted petals, which give the flower a contorted appearance. The genus name *Streptanthus* is derived from the Greek for "twisted flower," referring to the flower shape. On the open, rocky areas where shieldleaf usually grows, the clasping, round shield-shaped leaves often attract more attention than do the flowers themselves. The leaves are 1 to 3 inches across and turn yellow by the middle of the summer. Shieldleaf grows from the foothills to timberline.

Found in the Sierra Nevada and the mountains of northern California.

Western Wallflower   *Erysimum capitatum*

Shieldleaf   *Streptanthus tortuosus*   Shieldleaf   *Streptanthus tortuosus*

NIGHTSHADE FAMILY   Solanaceae

The nightshade family is well known because many of its members are important for food, medicine, or horticulture. The three thousand species of this
family are worldwide in distribution but are especially common in the tropics.
They are primarily herbaceous plants, but some tropical species are shrubby or
small trees. The leaves are generally simple and are alternate on the stems. The
flowers are often large and showy; the sepals and petals are in fives. As a group,
nightshades contribute greatly to the world's food supply, with members including the potato, tomato, and eggplant. Other important members of this
group include the tobacco and the petunia.

Purple Nightshade   *Solanum xantii*

Purple nightshade creates colorful bushlike vegetation along rocky roadsides
and grassy niches, its deep green foliage contrasting with its blue flowers. These
saucer-shaped flowers, a half-inch or more wide, are the texture of crinkled
crepe paper. The flowers are eventually replaced by pea-shaped, green berries.
The 1- to 2-inch leaves are gray and hairy, the foliage often forming compact
mats. This nightshade has many subspecies, inhabiting foothills and lower-
elevation woodlands, where it blooms in May, as well as higher elevations,
where it blooms in late July and August.

Found widely in California and in Baja California.

OAK FAMILY   Fagaceae

The oak family is primarily found in the Northern Hemisphere and consists
of woody trees and shrubs, some with evergreen leaves. Male and female flowers are separate, with the male flowers usually as catkins and the female flowers
in smaller clusters. The oak and chestnut are examples of members of this
family. Many different species of oak are found in the foothill areas of California.

Bush Chinquapin   *Chrysolepis sempervirens*

A bushy, evergreen shrub, chinquapin is less conspicuous when flowering than
when it has fruit. Related to the oaks of the foothills, chinquapin grows up to
6 feet tall. The 3-inch oblong leaves are evergreen. They are yellow-green
above and rusty beneath. The flowers, borne in elongated clusters or catkins,
can permeate the air with their pungent odor. The prickly burrs resemble
those of the chestnut, to which it is related. The burrs are brownish gold and
conspicuous during the latter part of the summer. They make attractive addi-
tions to most floral displays.

Chinquapin inhabits dry, rocky ridges and slopes, where it mingles with
the wild cherry, snowbush, and manzanita.

If you take the time to dig into the chinquapin burr, you'll find a nutlike
fruit, somewhat resembling a hazelnut. When ripe, usually in September or
October, this nut can taste very sweet. Up to three nuts may be found within
a single burr; however, often only one develops.

Found from southern California north to southern Oregon.

Purple Nightshade *Solanum xantii*

Bush Chinquapin *Chrysolepis sempervirens*

ORCHID FAMILY   Orchidaceae

Although not plentiful in temperate North America, the orchid family is one of the largest known. Found mainly in the tropics, where many species are epiphytes growing on tropical trees, the family has about eighteen thousand species. The flowers are very distinctive, although those native to California are much smaller than the commercial orchids or those that occur naturally in the tropics. The flowers have three sepals, which are usually inconspicuous, and three petals. The two lateral petals resemble each other, but the third is larger and forms a saclike, spurred, or spatulate lip.

Spotted Coralroot   *Corallorhiza maculata*

Coralroot derives its nourishment from the decaying material of other plants rather than producing its own sugar as green plants do. Coralroot stems are brown, yellow, or purple. The leaves have degenerated into small scales along the length of the stem. The underground stem is divided into short, knobby, coral-like pieces, responsible for the common name as well as the genus name.

Spotted coralroot can grow up to 30 inches tall, but more commonly reaches about 12 inches tall. The flowers are arranged loosely along the upper portion of the stem. The white lower lip is three-lobed and spotted with purple, a pattern that distinguishes this species. Spotted coralroot is quite common in damp conifer forests and blooms on the floor of sequoia groves in July. At higher elevations, it appears among the needles beneath mountain hemlock in early August.

Found widely in the Pacific states, east across North America to Newfoundland.

Striped Coralroot   *Corallorhiza striata*

Striped coralroot grows between 6 and 20 inches tall and has reddish or pale brown stems that emerge from the decomposing duff found on the floor of conifer forests at mid-elevations in the Sierra Nevada. The flowers are nearly 1 inch long and are pale yellow or pink with red or purple stripes, which results in the common name of this plant. To find striped coralroot requires careful searching—it usually grows in deep shade, and its coloration helps it blend with its surroundings.

Found in much of California north to British Columbia and east across northern North America; also found in northern Mexico.

Spotted Coralroot *Corallorhiza maculata*   **Striped Coralroot** *Corallorhiza striata*

Mountain Lady's Slipper   *Cypripedium montanum*

Mountain lady's slipper is one of those elusive wildflowers that is worth look-ing for. The plant grows 1 to 2 feet tall and has broad, deep green leaves that unfold as the plant matures. One flower petal is greatly expanded, forming a large, showy pouch that becomes the "slipper." It is a clean, smooth white color, although it may be prominently ribbed. The remaining floral parts are brown or purple, gracefully twisted and hanging over and behind the slipper.

Lady's slipper grows in the duff of conifer forests or on the slopes of mixed conifer and deciduous forests at mid-elevations. This elegant wildflower is becoming rare and should never be collected except by camera.

Found in the central and northern Sierra Nevada, north to Alaska and also in the northern Rocky Mountains.

Stream Orchid   *Epipactis gigantea*

Stream orchid is relatively common in the mixed conifer forest of the lower Sierra Nevada—but you must look diligently for it. It grows in seeps, along the edges of wet meadows, and on stream banks, where overhanging willows and other brush commonly keep it well hidden. Stream orchid's flowers are an inconspicuous bronze color that easily blends into the background vegetation. However, the delicate flowers are well worth the search. The green sepals are purple veined, and the lateral petals are pale purple or bronze with red veins. The lower lip is concave, resembling a long tongue sticking out. Several flow-ers cluster at the end of a stout stem 12 to 24 inches tall.

Found through much of California, north to British Columbia, and east to South Dakota and Texas.

Rattlesnake Plantain   *Goodyera oblongifolia*

A low rosette of deep green, leathery leaves, each with distinctive white mark-ings, quickly identifies the rattlesnake plantain. Because they are evergreen, these leaves may be seen at any time of year when the ground is free of snow. The waxy, white flowers open on the upper portion of a slender stalk that grows about 12 inches tall. This orchid grows, often in colonies, in dense, shaded conifer forests at lower and moderate elevations.

Found widely in the western United States and east across northern North America.

White-Flowered Bog Orchid   *Platanthera leucostachys*

A dense spike of white flowers with long spurs identifies this orchid, which inhabits boggy places through most of the Sierra Nevada. It typically grows along wet roadsides and lake margins, where it mingles with common camas and shooting stars. The linear leaves resemble those of the surrounding grasses and sedges. The thick, leafy stems grow 1 to 3 feet tall and bear half-inch-long white flowers near the tip. The upper petals of the flowers are arched, while the spurred lip is flat and reinlike.

Found widely across northern North America and in the western United States.

Similar species: Sparse-flowered bog orchid (*Platanthera sparsiflora*) is somewhat similar, but has fewer, green flowers spread along the upper por-tion of its 1- to 2-foot-tall stalk.

ountain Lady's Slipper *Cypripedium montanum*

Stream Orchid   *Epipactis gigantea*

Rattlesnake Plantain *Goodyera oblongifolia*
Inset: Rattlesnake Plantain flowers
Goodyera oblongifolia

White-Flowered Bog Orchid
Platanthera leucostachys

Ladies' Tresses   *Spiranthes romanzoffiana*

Resembling the finely braided hair of a well-coiffured lady, the greenish white flowers of this orchid form a spiral twist atop a 6- to 24-inch-tall stem. The genus name *Spiranthes,* derived from the Greek words meaning "coil" and "flower," refers to this trait. Ladies' tresses grows 6 to 12 inches tall, with mostly basal leaves. The tiny flowers cluster densely at the top of the stems. The flower parts fuse to form a vase, with one of the petals forming a protruding lip. Look for ladies' tresses along the margins of Angora Lake in the Eldorado National Forest and the wet places on Donner Pass.

Found widely in the Pacific states, east to New Mexico and east across northern North America.

Peony Family   Paeoniaceae

The peony family consists of small perennials that sprout from clustered, fleshy roots. The family has only one genus, which contains about thirty species. Two species grow in California, one in the Sierra Nevada and the other in coastal chaparral.

Peony   *Paeonia brownii*

Growing in scattered clumps in open woodlands, the peony has flowers that are fairly inconspicuous when they bloom in May and June. They resemble the garden peony but hang down from the stems, thereby blending in with the leaves and dry needles of the forest setting. The flowers have eight to thirteen petals. The petals are leathery, dull brown or reddish, and form a globular cup but fall off soon after the flower appears. The stems grow 1 to 2 feet tall but typically bend over when mature so that the seedpods rest on the ground. The leaves are somewhat succulent and are irregularly divided into narrow lobes.

This species of *Paeonia* was collected by explorer-botanist David Douglas in 1826 in the Blue Mountains of Oregon. Douglas was an avid collector of Northwestern plants. He made three separate trips to North America, sent by the Horticultural Society of London, which wanted new plants that could be cultivated in England. On his third trip, in 1830, he spent nearly two years crisscrossing California on his quest for new species that could be sent back to England.

Found in northern and central California north to British Columbia and east to Nevada and Wyoming.

Ladies' Tresses *Spiranthes romanzoffiana*   **Peony** *Paeonia brownii*

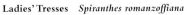

Phlox Family
Polemoniaceae

Nearly 320 species of plants belong to the phlox family. They are mostly annuals or perennial herbs. The flowers are often showy, with floral parts in fives. The united petals form a tubular corolla. Many garden varieties of phlox and gilia belong to this family.

Blue Gilia
Gilia capitata

Also called globe gilia, this plant heralds spring. An erect, annual plant, it grows on open slopes and meadows in foothills and pine forests. The deep blue or pale flowers are in dense, round clusters, sometimes containing up to a hundred individual flowers. They grow at the end of singular or branched stems 10 to 24 inches tall. The leaves are 1 to 4 inches long and divided into deeply notched, narrow lobes. The leaves are mostly at the base of the stem, although some greatly reduced leaves may also occur along the upper part of the stem.

Found from California and Baja California north to Idaho and British Columbia.

Scarlet Gilia
Ipomopsis aggregata

Also called skyrocket gilia and foxfire, this brightly colored wildflower is abundant in dry openings around Lake Tahoe in early July, covering many roadside banks with brilliant scarlet. Occasionally growing among blue lupines, the bright, tubular flowers make most other wildflowers seem pale. The inch-long floral tubes have narrow lobes that spread from the tip of the tube and flex almost backward. The protruding stamens add to its attractiveness. Growing from 1 to 4 feet tall, this gilia has leaves divided into narrow, linear lobes. When these brilliant flowers dominate an area, their mass effect is truly spectacular. Look for scarlet gilia if you visit the upper Truckee River area in the Eldorado National Forest, Snow Creek in Yosemite National Park, or Golden Trout Creek in the Inyo National Forest.

Found widely in the mountains of the western United States.

Blue Gilia *Gilia capitata*

Scarlet Gilia *Ipomopsis aggregata*

Mustang Clover   *Linanthus montanus*

Most members of the genus *Linanthus* have small, inconspicuous flowers; mustang clover is one of the more conspicuous. It grows 4 to 24 inches tall and has leaves deeply cleft into five to eleven linear lobes. The flowers, tucked amid coarse, bristly bracts, form a terminal head. The inch-long, funnel-shaped floral tube is purple or lilac, with a yellow throat and a dark spot on each floral lobe. It grows in open, gravelly spots and is particularly abundant in the Giant Forest of Sequoia National Park or near White Wolf in Yosemite National Park.

Found in the central and southern Sierra Nevada.

Similar species: A somewhat smaller plant, **whisker brush** *(Linanthus ciliatus)* has short, hairy 3- to 12-inch stems. The flowers are also in terminal heads surrounded by stiff, leaflike bracts. The tubular flowers are about a half-inch long, with small, round, rose or purple lobes and a yellow throat. **Harkness' linanthus** *(L. harknessii)* has slender stems about 6 inches tall. The paired leaves are divided into three to five palmate lobes, and tiny white, funnel-shaped pale blue flowers grace the top of the plant. **Nuttall's linanthus** *(L. nuttallii)* has numerous leafy stems, 6 to 12 inches tall. The opposite leaves, about a half-inch long, are divided to the base, making the leaves appear whorled. The half-inch-long, funnel-shaped, showy flowers are white or pale yellow, with a darker yellow throat. They are abundant at North Lake in the Inyo National Forest.

Spreading Phlox   *Phlox diffusa*

Spread over open rocky and sandy spots from moderate elevations to timberline, this phlox can carpet large areas with its pink, white, or lilac blossoms. The half-inch-wide flowers occur at the tips of short, branching stems that are densely covered with short, pointed leaves. Sometimes the flowers are so dense they completely cover the leaves beneath them. The woody, prostrate stems grow 4 to 12 inches long, forming thick mats. Depending on elevation, phlox blooms from June to August.

Found in the Sierra Nevada north into the high mountains of the Northwest.

Similar species: A plant that closely resembles the spreading phlox, **granite gilia** *(Leptodactylon pungens)* also grows on rocky slopes throughout the Sierra. It, too, is a compact, leafy plant. In phlox, however, the leaves are opposite each other on the stem and entire (without notches or lobes); *Leptodactylon* leaves are arranged alternately on the stems and are cleft into lobes. The flower is also different. Granite gilia has a funnel-shaped flower that is creamy white, yellow, or pink; phlox flower lobes spread abruptly, at right angles to the flower tube.

Mustang Clover *Linanthus montanus*

Spreading Phlox *Phlox diffusa*

Granite Gilia *Leptodactylon pungens*

Jacob's Ladder   *Polemonium californicum*

The dainty blue or violet flowers of this *Polemonium* are often found shyly
hiding in the shade of our conifer woodlands or in moist areas in the red fir,
lodgepole pine, and subalpine forest. The bell-shaped blooms, about a half-
inch long, are at the end of 4- to 8-inch stems, which may be either erect or
decumbent. The leaves are divided into ten to twenty leaflets, arranged opposite each other. This leaflet arrangement, reminiscent of a ladder, gave rise to
the common name. The upper leaflets are often partially joined together.

Found in the Sierra Nevada north in the mountains to Washington, Idaho,
and Montana.

Similar species: A taller *Polemonium* found in wet places in the Sierra is
Polemonium occidentale. Its solitary, erect stems grow 1 to 3 feet tall, and its
spreading, bell-shaped flowers are an inch across. It grows in moist areas in
mid-elevation forests.

Sky Pilot   *Polemonium eximium*

Thought by many to be the finest and most beautiful Sierra wildflower, sky
pilot is strictly a plant of the high country and rarely grows below 10,000 feet
elevation. Its crown of brightly colored, fragrant blue flowers draws attention
in its otherwise stark surroundings. On finding an extensive colony growing
amid the rocks of an alpine slope, one must wonder how the plants survive or
anchor themselves in the seemingly nonexistent soil. Finding sky pilot while
hiking in the high country is its own reward. Look for it near Kearsarge Pass in
the Inyo National Forest or near the summit of Mount Dana within Yosemite
National Park.

Sky pilot can be mistaken for no other wildflower and rarely has any com-
petition for its chosen habitat. Its deep blue flowers have rounded lobes and
are clustered in a circular ball. The leaves, 1 to 4 inches long, consist of numerous leaflets, all crowded on the elongate leaf so that it resembles a slender,
fuzzy caterpillar. These leaves are sticky and have a musky odor. You may notice the stems from the previous year's leaves near the base of the green growth.

Found in the central and southern Sierra Nevada. Sky pilot is endemic to
the high country of the Sierra Nevada, meaning it is a native plant with a very
restricted or limited range.

Jacob's Ladder *Polemonium californicum* Sky Pilot *Polemonium eximium*

Sky Pilot *Polemonium eximium*

PINK FAMILY   Caryophyllaceae

The pink family contains more than two thousand species throughout the world, although most inhabit northern, temperate areas. Generally, they are herbaceous plants with opposite, usually linear leaves. The floral parts are in fives. Familiar examples include the garden pink, chickweed, carnation, sweet william, and baby's breath. More than a dozen pinks grow in the Sierra Nevada.

California Indian Pink   *Silene californica*

Indian pink, one of the most colorful flowers in the Sierra, has 1- to 2-inch-wide brilliant scarlet blossoms. Five petals, each deeply cut into four lobes, accentuate this flower's beauty. These tattered edges may remind you of the cuts made by pinking shears and thus help you remember the common name. It grows 6 to 24 inches tall. Another diagnostic trait is the sticky secretion on the upper part of the stem. The material often enmeshes small insects and suggests the common name, catchfly.

California Indian pink inhabits lower-elevation pine forests. It blooms in early summer, though you may find it during August in some areas. Look for it in the Wawona area in Yosemite National Park or along the Mineral King Road.

Found through most of California north into Oregon.

Similar species: California Indian pink may be the most conspicuous, but two other pinks deserve mention. **Sargent's campion *(Silene sargentii)*** grows in crevices and rocky areas at upper elevations throughout much of the Sierra. It has white or rose-colored flowers and petals divided into two lobes, with each lobe having a small lateral lobe, instead of four equal-sized lobes. It is a tufted plant that grows only 4 to 5 inches tall. The flowers appear in July and August. Another species inhabiting rocky areas and dry slopes at higher elevations is **mountain campion *(S. bernardina).*** Its flowers are greenish white or tinged with red, and each flower lobe is deeply cleft into four to six lobes. It grows 6 to 18 inches tall.

PIPEVINE FAMILY   Aristolochiaceae

This distinctively aromatic family consists of more than six hundred species, found mainly in the tropics. Our species grow from woody vines or horizontal rhizomes.

Pipevine   *Aristolochia californica*

This semiwoody vine may grow to 10 or 12 feet long and twine over foothill shrubs and small trees. It has ovate or slightly heart-shaped leaves. The entire plant is softly hairy. The distinctive flower is 1 to 2 inches long and blooms in late winter or early spring. The sepals form a curved pipe-shaped tube. The flower tube is green or pale brown on the outside, with reddish veins on the inside. Pipevine dwells at lower elevations where it trails over brushy vegetation along streamsides and other moist areas, such as springs and seeps.

Found in the central and northern Coast Range, Central Valley, and Sierra Nevada foothills.

California Indian Pink   *Silene californica*

California Indian Pink   *Silene californica*

Pipevine   *Aristolochia californica*

Wild-Ginger   *Asarum hartwegii*

To find this interesting plant, look for the heart-shaped leaves amid the duff and debris of the forest floor. These deep green leaves, 3 to 6 inches wide, display beautiful white patterns along the veins. The stems emerge from a scaly rootstock and are usually prostrate, the leaves being 3 to 6 inches above the ground. The flowers themselves are dull purple or maroon and also grow close to the ground. The most conspicuous features of the flower, however, are the triangular, hairy lobes that taper into a tail extending an inch or more.

The rootstock is extremely aromatic, accounting for the reference to ginger in this plant's common name. The early settlers reputedly used an eastern species of *Asarum* as a ginger substitute. The ginger of commerce is prepared from the branching rootstocks of the common ginger of Asia and New Guinea, *Zingiber officinale,* which belongs to the ginger family, not the pipevine family.

Found in the Sierra Nevada north into southern Oregon.

Similar species: Lemmon's wild ginger *(Asarum lemmonii)* grows in moist places and it, too, has thin, heart-shaped leaves, but lacks tails on the floral lobes. Although it is found in most of the central and northern Sierra Nevada, it is not nearly as common as *Asarum hartwegii.*

POPPY FAMILY   **Papaveraceae**

The poppy family contains mostly annuals and perennials, although a few members are small trees or shrubs. There are about four hundred species. The flowers usually have two to four sepals, four or six petals, four or more stamens, and a single pistil. Many ornamental poppies grace our gardens. The plant yielding the drug opium belongs to this family.

Prickly Poppy   *Argemone munita*

Prickly poppy is particularly conspicuous on the sunny hillsides of the east slope of the Sierra in late July and August. Look for it when you drive over Monitor Pass in the Toiyabe National Forest. A stout plant, 2 to 4 feet tall, it has prickly stems and leaves. The large flowers, however, are the most notable feature. They are 2 to 5 inches across and have three to six floppy, white petals and a central cluster of yellow, orange, or red stamens, which can number from 150 to 250. When the central stamens are yellow, the massive flowers remind one of "eggs, sunny-side up."

Found from southern California and Arizona north to Nevada.

Wild-Ginger *Asarum hartwegii*   Inset: Wild-Ginger flower *Asarum hartwegii*

Lemmon's Wild-Ginger   *Asarum lemmonii*
Inset: Lemmon's Wild-Ginger flower   *Asarum lemmonii*

Prickly Poppy   *Argemone munita*

Bush Poppy
Dendromecon rigida

The bush poppy is one of the few woody members of the poppy family. It is a shrub growing 3 to 9 feet high with linear to oblong, evergreen leaves. When in bloom, it is attractive and catches the eye. The buttery yellow flowers are 1 to 3 inches across and borne at the ends of the branches, creating a golden halo around the bush.

Bush poppy was first described by the intrepid botanist David Douglas, who crisscrossed California in 1831–32. It is fairly common along roadways, dry washes and slopes, and recently disturbed areas at lower elevations in the southern part of the Sierra Nevada. It commonly is abundant after fires have burned foothill areas. Look for it along the entryways to Sequoia National Park, where it blooms in May.

Found from southern California south into Baja California.

Golden Eardrops
Dicentra chrysantha

Golden eardrops is a coarse-stemmed plant growing 2 to 6 feet tall. It produces a bright spire of erect, yellow flowers with four petals that form a blossom composed of two mirrored halves. The outer two petals form a pouch at the base, and the two inner petals are recurved toward the middle of the flower. They form a heart-shaped flower perched in loose clusters facing upward on the stems. The shiny, green leaves are finely dissected and up to a foot long, forming a delicate pattern.

Golden eardrops is abundant on dry slopes and often invades disturbed sites, such as roadsides or recently burned chaparral. It grows in the foothills up to about 5,000 feet elevation.

Found through much of California south into Baja California.

Bleedingheart
Dicentra formosa

Bleedingheart is easy to recognize. The pale purple or pink flowers consist of four petals that form a heart-shaped sac. They hang from a nodding stem that lifts them above the foliage. The leaves, too, are distinctive, each being finely divided, resembling a lacy doily or fernleaf.

Bleedingheart inhabits moist woodlands at moderate elevations, where it blooms during the spring and early part of the summer. In sheltered places bleedingheart may still be found blooming in late July. The plant spreads easily by underground stems and adapts well to cool areas of a native garden.

Found through much of California north to British Columbia.

Bush Poppy *Dendromecon rigida*   **Golden Eardrops** *Dicentra chrysantha*

Bleedingheart *Dicentra formosa*

Steer's head
Dicentra uniflora

Steer's head is one of the earliest of our native Sierran wildflowers to bloom. It inhabits the moist ground near retreating snowbanks. Although it is fairly widespread and not uncommon, it is often overlooked because of its small size. The four pink to white petals form a diminutive (barely a half-inch across) flower that resembles the head of a steer—hence the common name. The one or two leaves, which lie flat against the ground, are only an inch or two long. They are divided two or three times.

Steer's head grows on sandy or gravelly places in openings within upper-elevation forests to timberline.

Found in the mountains of California north to Washington and into the northern Rocky Mountains.

California Poppy
Eschscholzia californica

Golden fields of poppies are a common sight in the Sierra foothills in spring and summer. This colorful wildflower usually grows in patches or extensive openings, always in full sunlight, and is quick to invade waste areas—roadsides, dry washes, and lightly grazed hillsides. Originally, the California poppy ranged from near the Columbia River to Baja California and Arizona. Widely planted as a garden flower, it has escaped cultivation and now grows at lower elevations throughout most of the western United States.

Growing 1 to 2 feet tall, individual poppy plants are compact, their many stems and leaves giving a bushy appearance. A variable species in the wild, its flowers range in color from a buttery yellow to a crimson golden orange. Some cultivated varieties have petals that are deep orange at the base, blending into a brilliant yellow at the edge. The attractive bluish green leaves are divided several times into linear or oblong lobes. When the buds first appear, the outer flower parts form a pointed cap over the petals. As the petals unfold, they push the cap off.

This little flower has attracted much attention because of its abundance and loveliness. Californians selected it as their state flower in 1890, making it one of the first recognized state flowers in the Union. The early Spanish settlers called it *copa de ora* or "cup of gold." According to their beliefs, the orange gold petals turn to gold, falling and filling the soil with the metal so eagerly sought by the miners of 1849. Another early name for the poppy was *dormidera,* meaning "sleepy one," because the flowers close at night. On cloudy days, they may only partially open or even remain closed.

The California poppy was named by botanist Adelbert von Chamisso, who visited California in the winter of 1816–17 when aboard the Russian ship *Rurik.* Landing in San Francisco Bay, Chamisso and the ship's doctor, Johann Friedrich Gustav von Eschscholtz, found the brightly colored flowers. Chamisso named the plant for his friend.

Found through most of California north into southern Washington, east into Nevada, and south into New Mexico and northern Baja California.

Steer's head *Dicentra uniflora*

California Poppy *Eschscholzia californica*

PRIMROSE FAMILY   Primulaceae

The primrose family contains about six hundred species of plants, most of which live in the Northern Hemisphere. They are annual or perennial herbs with simple leaves and flowers with floral parts generally in fours or fives. The petals are usually reflexed or spreading, making attractive blossoms. Many primroses have become cultivated.

Jeffrey Shooting Star   *Dodecatheon jeffreyi*

Recognize shooting stars by their four or five purple petals, united at the base but divided into linear segments that curve back over the rest of the flower, exposing the erect stamens. Jeffrey shooting star grows 1 to 2 feet tall in wet mountain meadows and has a basal cluster of leaves, each from 2 to 15 inches long. Five to fifteen nodding flowers grace the top of each stem.

Jeffrey shooting star graces wet or damp meadows, stream banks, and lakeshores at middle to upper elevations. Often locally abundant, they can cover a meadow with their purple flowers. Good places to see this shooting star include Tuolumne Meadows in Yosemite National Park and the Winnemucca Lake area in the Eldorado National Forest.

Found in the Sierra Nevada and northwestern part of California north to Alaska and Montana.

Similar species: Alpine shooting star *(Dodecatheon alpinum)* is much smaller, about 12 inches tall. It has strap-shaped leaves 1 to 5 inches long and grows in moist meadows throughout the middle elevation Sierra forest, not just at upper elevations. The two species can be distinguished by close examination of the individual flower stems. Jeffrey shooting star has small glands or hairs, while alpine shooting star does not. At higher elevations in the southern Sierra, you may encounter **D. redolens.** It is quite glandular and grows between 10 and 24 inches tall. Its flowers have five stamens; the other shooting stars discussed here usually have four stamens.

Sierra Primrose   *Primula suffrutescens*

Seeing a patch of these rose or purple flowers is breathtaking. Composed of a floral tube with a yellow throat and five widely spreading, deeply notched lobes, the flowers are on a leafless stalk, 1 to 4 inches high. The evergreen leaves, clustered at the base, are wedge-shaped, toothed at the tip, and about an inch long. The blossoms of Sierra primrose wave in the mountain breeze, usually not far from a retreating snowbank. Sierra primrose might even be considered "snowbank dependent." It most often dwells in a north-facing, protected ravine or hollow, where it depends on the slowly melting snow for constant moisture.

Sierra primrose is an erratically distributed plant. More common in the southern Sierra, for instance along the trail to Kearsarge Pass in the Inyo National Forest, it usually grows in isolated colonies. However, each colony may be extensive and contain hundreds of plants. Although the primrose is less common in the northern Sierra Nevada, it inhabits places such as Basin Peak near Donner Pass and Round Lake in the Plumas National Forest.

Found in the Sierra Nevada north into the Klamath Range.

Jeffrey Shooting Star   *Dodecatheon jeffreyi*   Jeffrey Shooting Star   *Dodecatheon jeffreyi*

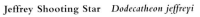

Sierra Primrose   *Primula suffrutescens*
Inset: Sierra Primrose flower   *Primula suffrutescens*

Purslane Family   Portulacaceae

The purslane family contains about four hundred species of plants that are either annuals or perennials and are distributed mostly in moderate climates. The leaves can be either alternate or opposite on the stem and are often fleshy or succulent. The flowers have two sepals and four or more petals. The family contains some lovely garden plants such as the rosemoss.

Pussypaws   *Calyptridium umbellatum*

Anyone who explores the Sierra in midsummer will undoubtedly see pussypaws. This common plant flourishes on the dry sandy soils and gravels found along trails and roadsides. Pussypaws responds to the warmth and light of the sun. In the morning and evening hours it will hug the earth, its reddish stems pressed flat against the ground. By midday, the stems will be nearly upright. At lower elevations, the prone plants may be 8 to 10 inches across, while at higher elevations they are much smaller, being only 2 to 3 inches in diameter. The pinkish flowers are borne in dense clusters at the tips of the stems. The basal leaves, arranged flat on the ground in a rosette, have a leathery texture and are somewhat elongate.

The name *pussypaws* seems appropriate for this little purslane. If you look carefully at a cluster of flowers, you'll see that it closely resembles the furred paws of a kitten. Cup a cluster of flowers between your thumb and fingers, and you'll feel the softness of a kitten's paw. Chipmunks and other small rodents eagerly consume the black, shiny seeds that appear toward the end of the summer.

Found in mountainous areas of the western United States, north into British Columbia.

Miner's Lettuce   *Claytonia perfoliata*

The dainty flowers of this purslane have five quarter-inch, pale pink or white petals and two green sepals. However, you will most easily recognize miner's lettuce by the arrangement of the two small leaves on the otherwise bare stem. These are united to form a saucer or cup one-half to 2 inches in diameter beneath the cluster of flowers. Miner's lettuce is 4 to 10 inches tall and grows in brushy areas along most streams and on the floor of ponderosa pine and red fir forests wherever it is shady and damp. The flowers bloom from April to June.

As the common name implies, the miners who swarmed the foothills in their quest for gold found this plant to be valuable. It was used as a salad green not only by the miners but also by the early settlers and, even earlier, by American Indians. The raw leaves are good to nibble as you walk along a quiet mountain path.

Found widely in the western states, north into British Columbia.

Pussypaws   *Calyptridium umbellatum*

Miner's Lettuce   *Claytonia perfoliata*

Dwarf Lewisia
Lewisia pygmaea

Dwelling only in the higher-elevation basins and slopes, this little wildflower is often overlooked by hikers who explore the Sierra high country in June and July. A low-growing plant, it hugs the ground, the linear basal leaves sprouting from a thick, fleshy root (characteristic of many *Lewisia*) and extending beyond the flowering stems. The pink or white flower, consisting of six to eight petals, is about one-half inch in diameter. Dwarf lewisia grows in soil kept moist by nearby melting snow and may conspicuously dot an area one week, only to disappear by the next.

Found in the mountains of California north to British Columbia and also in the Rocky Mountains.

Similar species: Very similar, **Nevada lewisia** *(Lewisia nevadensis)* also thrives in moist soil. However, it may grow at lower elevations, too, particularly in ponderosa pine forests in the springtime. Where dwarf lewisia and Nevada lewisia occur together, you can distinguish them by looking carefully at the two sepals, located beneath the floral petals. The sepals of dwarf lewisia are toothed and have purple glands, almost appearing purple-fringed. Those of Nevada lewisia are not fringed or glandular.

Bitterroot
Lewisia rediviva

The bitterroot grows in a wide variety of habitats—stony slopes, gravelly benches, and rocky crevices; in open pine and juniper forests; or on sagebrush scrubland. It may vary in color and size from one location to another. This low-growing, succulent herb produces large, conspicuous blossoms in spring. The numerous sepals and petals, all somewhat alike, are a half-inch to an inch long and range from rose or purple to pale pink or white. The succulent, linear leaves usually dry up and shrivel by the time the flowers open, leaving the blooming bitterroot to appear as though it lacks leaves entirely.

The bitterroot was first collected by Captain Meriwether Lewis of the famed Lewis and Clark Expedition of 1804–6. As they crossed the northern plains and western mountains by way of the Missouri and Columbia River systems, the captains made extensive collections of plants, which were later dispersed to several botanists of the day. Lewis observed bitterroot when in the company of the Shoshone Indians, who used it as a food staple. Other early botanists noted that bitterroot was so valuable that a sack of them might be traded for a horse. Bitterroot is now the state flower of Montana.

Found widely in the mountains of western North America.

Similar species: Two other bitterroots with large, attractive flowers deserve mention. **Yosemite bitterroot** *(Lewisia disepala)* blooms in local abundance on the rocky rims of the Yosemite Valley. It has two conspicuous petal-like sepals. The flowering stems are shorter than the fleshy, linear leaves, and each bears a single white or pink flower composed of two sepals and five to seven petals. **Kellogg's lewisia** *(L. kelloggii)* has rosettes of thick, spatulate leaves and conspicuous, cream-colored flowers. The blossoms, tucked among the leaves, are sessile and have a pair of sepal-like bracts. The sepals are oblong, with toothed margins. Kellogg's lewisia grows on sandy ridgetops and decomposed granite in the subalpine and mixed conifer forests of the Sierra Nevada.

Dwarf Lewisia *Lewisia pygmaea*

Bitterroot *Lewisia rediviva*   Inset: Bitterroot *Lewisia rediviva*

Kellogg's Lewisia *Lewisia kelloggii*

Rose Family
Rosaceae

This large family contains trees, shrubs, and herbaceous plants. It is a world-wide group containing some three thousand species. They have mostly alternate leaves, which may be simple or compound. The flowers are usually in five parts with numerous stamens. Many species of the rose family have showy, conspicuous flowers. The rose family plays an important economic role, containing such food plants as apples, plums, pears, strawberries, cherries, and raspberries.

Serviceberry
Amelanchier alnifolia

When serviceberry is in bloom, it is a beautiful shrub. It may be compact or scraggly, a few feet tall or a small tree growing 20 feet tall. The flowers have five narrow white petals that are usually twisted, giving a somewhat ragged appearance to each blossom. The oval leaves, from 1 to 2 inches long, are roughly toothed, especially on the upper half. Serviceberry grows in small openings in the red fir and lodgepole pine forests and on open slopes and scrubland. Where it is plentiful on open hillsides, its blossoms form a beautiful springtime display.

The round, berrylike fruits are deep blue, with a whitish bloom or coating. Botanically, they are similar to apples, with bits of the flower still attached to the top of each fruit. Although many modern taste buds consider the fruits too mealy and sweet, explorers and miners found them a welcome addition to their otherwise bland and limited diet. Early settlers learned to make fine jellies, jams, pies, and wines from the serviceberry. Many Indians of western North America held the plant in high esteem; the berries were a staple of their diet. They pressed dried berries into small cakes, which were later added as flavoring in stews and soups. The dried berries were also pounded into dried meat for carrying on long trips. The small fruits are now eaten mainly by wild animals; pheasants, grouse, coyotes, and rabbits feast on them.

Serviceberry plays an important role in the natural plant community. It often grows in dense patches and covers hillsides and slopes, where it helps control erosion.

Found widely in northern and western North America.

Curl-Leaf Mountain Mahogany
Cercocarpus ledifolius

Mountain mahoganies are most conspicuous when their feathery-tailed fruits, not their flowers, are present. The genus name refers to this characteristic: *Cercocarpus* is derived from the Greek *karpos,* "fruit." The common name refers to the mountain habitat where it normally grows, usually on dry slopes or ridges, and the plant's hard, reddish wood.

Mountain mahogany has clustered leaves that are evergreen and leathery, with the edges rolled under. A densely branched shrub or small tree, it has small greenish or cream-colored flowers that lack petals. Growing from moderate elevations nearly to timberline, mountain mahogany blooms from April to May, depending on elevation and exposure. You'll see the silvery plumed seeds adorning these shrubs at Monitor Pass in the Toiyabe National Forest in early August, although at lower elevations mountain mahogany may be fruiting by June.

Found from California and Arizona north to Montana and eastern Washington and east to Wyoming and Utah.

Similar species: Birchleaf mountain mahogany *(Cercocarpus betuloides)* is common in many foothill areas. Its leaves are not rolled inward along their edges but instead resemble those of the birch tree.

Serviceberry   *Amelanchier alnifolia*

Curl-Leaf Mountain Mahogany   *Cercocarpus ledifolius*

Mountain Misery
Chamaebatia foliolosa

This small shrub has a number of local names: bearmat, bear-clover, fern bush, tarweed, and kit-kit-dizzy. Mountain misery is a low-growing, resinous shrub with fernlike, pinnnately divided, evergreen leaves. It forms small patches or extensive mats. In some areas, it may be the only undergrowth, its extensive root system and dense foliage making it difficult for other plants to become established. Mountain misery grows 1 to 2 feet tall and forms tangled undergrowth that is hard to walk through. The sticky, strong-smelling resin found on the leaves clings to clothing, accounting for the common name, mountain misery. The strong scent resembles that of witch hazel. Five-petaled, white flowers, clustered at the ends of the young shoots, bloom in the early part of the summer and can be seen in June and July along the roadside near the Big Oak Flat entrance to Yosemite National Park.

Mountain misery grows in the partial shade of dry ponderosa or sugar pine forests along the western slopes of the Sierra Nevada.

Found in the Sierra Nevada and southern Cascade Range.

Similar species: Fern bush *(Chamaebatiaria millefolium)* also has finely divided, fernlike leaves and aromatic foliage. However, it grows only on the eastern slopes of the Sierra Nevada.

Mountain Strawberry
Fragaria virginiana

Wild strawberries are low-growing, perennial herbs with scaly, underground rootstocks. They generally produce runners, or stolons, which creep across the ground and root at the tips, producing a new plant. Wild strawberries have numerous basal leaves, composed of three leaflets that are toothed and long petioles. This wild strawberry has truncated leaflets. The white flowers are about 1 inch in diameter and produce a sweet-tasting, small red fruit by midsummer. At lower elevations the flowers bloom from March to June. However, a few blooms may still be found at higher elevations in July. You'll find them in the partial shade of forest openings.

The fruit of the wild strawberry is a rare sight, even though the ground in some places may be covered with white strawberry blossoms in the spring and early summer. Birds and small rodents so eagerly seek the berries that few ever reach the human palate. Not so well known, however, is the value of strawberry leaves, which produce one of the better wild teas. Fresh leaves can be steeped in hot water or dried for future use.

Found widely through California and northern and eastern North America. Also found in Europe.

Similar species: Wood strawberry *(Fragaria vesca)* inhabits meadows and forest openings, from lower elevations to timberline. You can distinguish these two strawberries by looking closely at the leaves. In mountain strawberry the leaflets have fewer than thirteen teeth, and the tip of the center leaflet is truncated, as if it had been cut flat across the top. In wood strawberry the central leaflet has between twelve and twenty-one teeth and is rounded at the tip.

Mountain Misery *Chamaebatia foliolosa*

Mountain Strawberry *Fragaria virginiana*

Cream Bush
Holodiscus microphyllus

The rose family has a number of beautiful flowering shrubs. Also called rock spirea, this one grows at middle and upper elevations in the Sierra Nevada, sometimes at timberline. It may grow 3 feet tall where conditions are favorable, but more often it is a smaller, almost scraggly shrub. It has alternate, wedge-shaped, toothed leaves and is covered with plumes of small white or cream-colored flowers. Although these plumes of flowers are at the ends of the branches, they are generally mixed with the leafy branches and do not extend beyond them.

Found from Baja California northward in the Sierra Nevada to southern Oregon, east into the central Rocky Mountains.

Similar species: Ocean spray *(Holodiscus discolor)* is a taller shrub that grows up to 20 feet tall and is found at lower elevations in the mountains and also on the coast. It, too, has a spray of cream-colored or white flowers, but they extend beyond the leafy branches, forming graceful, hanging plumes.

Dusky Horkelia
Horkelia fusca

Horkelia is a perennial herb with white flowers in tight, terminal clusters. The five wedge-shaped petals of each blossom emerge from a cuplike base. Horkelia grows 6 to 20 inches tall. Most of the leaves are basal and are pinnately compound with ten to thirty leaflets crowded together. Growing in open woodlands and slopes and at the edge of dry meadows, it is quite variable, with many closely related forms throughout the Sierra.

Found in the Sierra Nevada north into Washington and east into the Great Basin.

Mousetails
Ivesia santolinoides

Mousetails is a tufted, silky-looking plant. The small, white flowers form open, branched clusters atop stems that are 6 to 18 inches tall. The characteristic most people note, however, is not the flowers but the basal leaves. Up to 4 inches long, they are pinnately compound, and the tiny leaflets overlap each other. They also are covered with dense, silky hairs and thereby resemble a mouse's tail.

Mousetails grows in open lodgepole pine and red fir forests, as well as subalpine areas, usually in hot, dry openings.

Found in the upper elevations of the Sierra Nevada and also in some mountain ranges of southwestern California.

Similar species: Club-moss ivesia *(Ivesia lycopodioides)* is a yellow-flowered plant often growing in the company of dusky horkelia in open woodlands and meadows. It has yellow flowers and nearly leafless, 2- to 12-inch-tall stems that may be either erect or sprawling. The basal leaves are 1 to 6 inches long and divided into twenty to fifty leaflets, which are in turn divided almost to the base. These tufted leaves resemble clumps of moss, hence the common name.

Cream Bush *Holodiscus microphyllus*   **Dusky Horkelia** *Horkelia fusca*

Mousetails *Ivesia santolinoides*   **Club-Moss Ivesia** *Ivesia lycopodioides*

CINQUEFOILS
Potentilla species

Members of this genus are sometimes confused with the buttercup genus, *Ranunculus,* because both have yellow flowers with five petals. Close inspection, however, will show the differences. Cinquefoils have five golden yellow petals that alternate with five green sepals located below them. Five shorter bracts alternate with the sepals. Buttercups lack these bracts between the sepals (see page 26). Cinquefoils have compound leaves that are either pinnately or palmately compound. Palmately compound leaves have leaflets that originate from a common point. Pinnately compound leaves have leaflets arranged along a linear line. More than twenty-five species of *Potentilla* grow in the Sierra Nevada. Only a few of the most common will be treated here.

Drummond's Cinquefoil
Potentilla drummondii

Drummond's cinquefoil is a somewhat tufted plant with stems that may be either erect or sprawling. The stems are 4 to 24 inches long and bear leaves with four to eighteen leaflets that may be deeply cleft or merely toothed or lobed. The leaves are sometimes crowded together and may be covered with dense, silky hairs. *Potentilla drummondii* is a variable species with many sub-species, which display either densely hairy leaves or green, hairless leaves. Drummond's cinquefoil is a common component of moist mountain meadows and rocky basins from mid-elevations up to timberline.

Found widely in the mountains of western North America.

Similar species: Fan-foil *(Potentilla flabellifolia)* is also found at higher elevations and grows up to 12 inches tall. The leaves of this species remind one of the strawberry—three wedge-shaped leaflets comprise a leaf.

Cinquefoil
Potentilla gracilis

This cinquefoil is one of the more common and widespread. It is typically a tufted plant, growing from a thick rhizome. About one-half inch across, the flowers of this species are attractive. The five bright yellow floral petals are somewhat heart-shaped, with a small notch in the outer edge. The leaves are mostly basal and are palmately divided into five to seven leaflets, meaning each of the leaflets originates from a common point, like the fingers of a hand. This cinquefoil is quite variable, growing 15 to 30 inches tall, from lowland areas to timberline. Generally, it prefers moist places such as stream banks and wet meadows.

Found widely in western North America.

Similar species: Sticky cinquefoil *(Potentilla glandulosa)* has pinnately compound leaves, meaning the leaflets are arranged on both sides of the petiole or leaf stalk. Growing up to 30 inches tall, this cinquefoil grows in dry or moist openings. The flowers are pale yellow rather than the bright golden yellow of *P. gracilis.* Although usually found at moderate and lower elevations, it is known to range up to 12,000 feet elevation.

Drummond's Cinquefoil *Potentilla drummondii*
Inset: Drummond's Cinquefoil showing hairless leaf form *Potentilla drummondii*

Fan-Foil *Potentilla flabellifolia*   Cinquefoil *Potentilla gracilis*

Shrubby Cinquefoil
Potentilla fruticosa

A woody shrub, this cinquefoil is common in some alpine areas and lodge-pole pine forests. It grows 1 to 4 feet tall and has leaves composed of three to seven narrow leaflets. Since it is the only woody cinquefoil known to inhabit the Sierra Nevada, it is easily identified. Shrubby cinquefoil is especially conspicuous when the bright yellow flowers are blooming.

The name *cinquefoil* is probably derived from the French word *cinque,* "five," and the medieval English word *foil,* "leaf." This refers to the five fingerlike leaflets characteristic of many of the genus.

Found widely in the mountains of western North America and across northern North America.

Bitter Cherry
Prunus emarginata

The bitter cherry is named for its small fruits or cherries, which are intensely bitter even when fully ripe. The five-petaled, white flowers bloom in round-topped clusters in April and May. Dark green oblong leaves with fine-toothed edges occur alternately on the stems. The bright red cherry appears in late summer or early fall and contains juicy pulp. Although bitter cherry may attain the size of a small tree, it is more often a spreading, crooked-branched shrub 3 to 10 feet tall. The bark has a distinctly cherry odor when bruised.

Bitter cherry grows in open brush fields, along rocky slopes and ravines, and openings in dry woodlands and coniferous forests. It is usually found in the company of whitethorn, manzanita, and serviceberry and can be seen along most roadsides entering Sierra national forests and parks.

Found widely in the mountains of the western United States.

Similar species: Also blooming in April and May, the **Sierra plum** *(Prunus subcordata)* resembles bitter cherry. However, its fruits are reddish purple and the leaves are rounded. In addition, the branches may have small, spinelike twigs on them. Sierra plum fruits make excellent jams and jellies.

Western Chokecherry
Prunus virginiana

Western chokecherry is an erect shrub or small tree that rarely reaches 20 feet in height. Its white flowers form 2- to 4-inch-long showy, elongated clusters at the end of leafy branches. The individual flowers have five white petals and numerous stamens. The leaves are alternate on the stems, 1 to 3 inches long, with pointed tips and toothed edges. The berries are dark purple or black, with a puckery taste. These grapelike clusters of fruit are attractive, as well as utilitarian. They are a favored food source for many birds and small rodents. Although tart, they make good jellies, jams, and wine.

Chokecherry inhabits sunny places, commonly along streams in fairly open valleys or in sunny canyons. It also grows near springs and seeps in sandy soils and occasionally on rocky talus slopes as well.

Found widely in California, also in the Great Basin and central Great Plains.

Shrubby Cinquefoil *Potentilla fruticosa*

Western Chokecherry fruits *Prunus virginiana*
Inset: Western Chokecherry flowers
Prunus virginiana

Bitter Cherry *Prunus emarginata*

Bitterbrush
Purshia tridentata

Also called antelope bush, quinine bush, and black sage, bitterbrush is a semierect shrub that is widely distributed in arid regions of the western states. It grows from 1 to 6 feet tall, depending on local conditions. In the spring, a mass display of bitterbrush's 1-inch-wide yellow flowers attracts attention to this generally inconspicuous plant. Each showy flower has five spatulate petals and numerous stamens. The clustered leaves are three-toothed at the tip and slightly less than 1 inch long. They are wedge-shaped, with rolled-under margins. In open places on the east side of the Sierra Nevada, bitterbrush may dominate large areas. It also is often the main shrub understory of open pine forests. On Carson Pass in the Eldorado National Forest, it is a scraggly shrub—barely reaching a foot tall—and blooms in early July.

The generic name *Purshia* honors Frederick T. Pursh (1774–1820), a distinguished botanical explorer and author. The shrub, however, was first collected by Captain Meriwether Lewis. The descriptive name *tridentata* refers to the leaves, which are three-toothed, or tridentate. Bitterbrush is an appropriate common name because of the taste of the leaves. Nonetheless, it is one of the most important browse plants in the western states, enjoyed by both domestic and wild animals.

Found widely in western North America.

Wood's Rose
Rosa woodsii

Members of the genus *Rosa* are erect, trailing, or climbing shrubs, often with prickly stems. They have alternate leaves that are usually compound, and the leaflets have toothed edges. The five floral petals (rarely four, six, seven, or eight) are red, pink, or sometimes yellow. The fleshy, round fruit, known as a "hip," is red and rich in vitamin C. The hip makes a tasty jelly or, chopped and steeped in hot water, a good tea.

Wood's rose is a stout, erect shrub, 3 to 9 feet tall. Its leaflets are almost 1 inch across and pleasantly scented, as are the 1- to 2-inch-wide flowers. One of our most attractive wild roses, it grows in damp coniferous forests, particularly in the eastern Sierra.

Found widely in the western United States.

Thimbleberry
Rubus parviflorus

Thimbleberry is one of the most widespread members of this genus, which includes the wild and cultivated blackberries and raspberries. It has showy, white flowers with five petals, which are thin and crinkled like crepe paper. The leaves are alternate on the stem, 3 to 12 inches wide, and have three to five pointed lobes.

Thimbleberry grows on moist, shaded sites, along streams and cool draws, and on wooded hillsides under open clumps of ponderosa and lodgepole pine. Sometimes forming dense, almost solid stands, it is a conspicuous plant when blooming in June and July. The name *thimbleberry* is derived from the shape of the juicy, reddish fruit, resembling the cultivated raspberry. It provides a refreshing but rather bland snack for hikers.

Thimbleberry was first collected and named by the botanist Thomas Nuttall (see page 40) on the shores of Lake Huron.

Found widely in western and northern North America.

Bitterbrush *Purshia tridentata*   Inset: Bitterbrush flowers *Purshia tridentata*

Wood's Rose   *Rosa woodsii*

Thimbleberry   *Rubus parviflorus*

Sibbaldia
Sibbaldia procumbens

Sibbaldia is a low, matted perennial that could almost be mistaken for a wild strawberry. It has creeping stems, and each leaf is divided into three wedge-shaped leaflets. The tip of each leaflet has three prominent teeth. The five-petaled flowers, however, are yellow, not white as in wild strawberry, and each petal is very slender. The petals alternate with prominent sepals and have bracts beneath them. You must look carefully for sibbaldia—its diminutive size makes it easy to overlook. It grows in moist, rocky areas or openings at mid and upper elevations.

Found in scattered areas of California and across northern North America; also in Europe and Asia.

Mountain Ash
Sorbus scopulina

Mountain ash is a conspicuous shrub wherever it dwells in the Sierra. In June it is adorned with flat-topped clusters of white flowers. Later in the summer and early fall, the leaves turn brilliant red, and the flowers are replaced by bright orange or scarlet berrylike fruit. This mountain ash grows to 15 feet or so in height. Its leaves have nine to thirteen leaflets, which are lance-shaped or oblong. Mountain ash thrives in damp, wooded areas.

Where mountain ash is common, it may be an important food plant, as both domestic animals and wild game eat the tender twigs. The ripe berries are also used as food by many species of birds. Gregarious Steller's and gray jays will quickly consume the fruit of an entire tree.

Found in the Sierra Nevada north into British Columbia and also in the Rocky Mountains.

Similar species: California mountain ash *(Sorbus californica)* is a smaller shrub, growing 3 to 6 feet high. Its compound leaves have seven to nine leaflets.

Mountain Spiraea
Spiraea densiflora

The spiraeas are attractive flowering shrubs with simple leaves, arranged alternately on the stems. Native spiraeas have tiny flowers, crowded into showy clusters that may be round-topped or elongated. This species has rose- or pink-colored flowers. Growing up to 3 feet tall, mountain spiraea's slender stems grow close together, forming a dense, compact shrub. The flowers themselves are fragrant and dainty. The stamens are longer than the other floral parts, giving a fuzzy effect to the floral cluster. Showy plants when in bloom, spireas add to the beauty of many of our mountain slopes.

Blooming from July through August, mountain spiraea grows at moderate and upper elevations, usually on moist, rocky slopes.

Found from California north to British Columbia and east into Wyoming and Montana.

Sibbaldia   *Sibbaldia procumbens*

Mountain Ash   *Sorbus scopulina*
Inset: Mountain Ash fruit   *Sorbus scopulina*   **Mountain Spiraea**   *Spiraea densiflora*

St. John's Wort Family   Hypericaceae

The St. John's wort family is a worldwide group consisting of annuals, perennials, and a few small trees. There are about four hundred species. A few are cultivated as garden plants. This family has attained some notoriety for its medicinal value as a sedative and antidepressant. A European member of this family, Klamath weed *(Hypericum perforatum)* is now an aggressive weed in western pastures and rangelands.

Tinker's Penny   *Hypericum anagalloides*

Tinker's penny is a delightful little plant, sometimes overlooked because of its diminutive size. This trailing plant, from 2 to 7 inches long, forms small mats in wet meadows, springs, and seeps. Its stems creep along the ground and grow from stolons that can root at the nodes. Occasionally the stems stand erect. Tinker's penny has glistening, green leaves that are only a half-inch long and ovate in shape. The leaves are opposite each other and sit tightly clasping the stems. The bright golden flowers have five petals and are about a half-inch in diameter.

Tinker's penny grows best where the ground is saturated, so you should plan on getting your feet and knees wet when you look for it. The leaves appear wet with dew; however, this is more likely because of secretions from small glands found on them rather than moisture.

Because tinker's penny spreads so readily from the creeping stems, it makes a nice addition to a wildflower garden. It adapts well to cool, moist nooks where it can be well watered.

Found through much of California north to British Columbia and east to Montana and Nevada.

St. John's Wort   *Hypericum formosum*

Common in meadows and along stream banks, St. John's wort is known for its five-petaled yellow flowers, accentuated by slender, erect stamens. The flowers, about a half-inch wide, cluster loosely at the upper ends of the stems, which grow 10 to 20 inches tall. This species has oblong, inch-long leaves that are dotted with black spots along the margins.

St. John's wort grows in damp openings within mid-elevation coniferous forests, such as seeps, springs, lake borders, and similar places where it can get full sunlight. It blooms from June through August.

Not native, but now found widely in California north into Canada and east to Colorado.

St. John's Wort *Hypericum formosum*

Tinker's Penny *Hypericum anagalloides*

Saxifrage Family   Saxifragaceae

The saxifrage family contains about six hundred species, many of which grow in northern climates. The scientific name means "rock-breaker," presumably because many of the plants inhabit high-elevation rocky outcrops or wet crevices on the sides of cliffs. Members of this family commonly have small flowers with four or five sepals and four or five petals. They are mostly herbaceous plants with alternate or basal leaves that are palmately veined.

Indian Rhubarb   *Darmera peltata*

Indian rhubarb grows 1 to 3 feet tall and has white or pink flowers, arranged loosely in a round-topped cluster. The large leaves, usually cupped in the center, may grow as wide as 2 feet, reaching their greatest development after the flowers have passed. Indian rhubarb grows along fast-moving streams in lower montane and subalpine forests and blooms from April to June.

The name *Indian rhubarb* refers to the edible young stalks, somewhat resembling celery in taste and texture. The older shoots can also be boiled and eaten.

Found in the Sierra Nevada north into southwestern Oregon.

Alumroot   *Heuchera rubescens*

This little alumroot is a highly variable species that intergrades with several other members of the genus. It is a dainty plant that frequents rocky cliffs and crevices at higher elevations. It has 12-inch-tall stems and clusters of hairy-stemmed, rounded, 1-inch-long basal leaves. The tiny, cup-shaped flowers are white or pale pink and appear to dance in the continuous alpine breeze. Most alumroots have stout, woody bases or underground rootstocks, many of which have an alumlike taste, resulting in the common name.

Found widely in the mountains of California and other western states.

Similar species: The more robust **small-flowered heuchera (***Heuchera micrantha***)** grows in sheltered rocky areas at lower elevations. Its flowering stems grow 12 to 24 inches tall.

Mitrewort   *Mitella breweri*

Also called bishop's cap, this odd-looking flower is easily overlooked because of its small size and green flowers. The petals are dissected into narrow lobes, giving a very delicate, almost fernlike appearance to the individual petals. Mitrewort grows about 12 inches tall. It has basal leaves that are 2 to 3 inches wide and round or heart-shaped, with slightly wavy edges. The leaf stems usually have curved, reddish hairs. The fruit or capsule resembles a mitre (headband or cap worn by a bishop), giving rise to both the common and generic names.

Look for these tiny flowers in damp, shaded places from June to August, depending on elevation. In June they may be blooming on the floor of a mid-elevation ponderosa pine forest, while in August they will still be found beside a mountain hemlock or western white pine near timberline, thriving on the moisture from a melting snowbank.

Found in the mountains of California, north into British Columbia and Montana, east into the mountains of Nevada.

Indian Rhubarb   *Darmera peltata*

Alumroot   *Heuchera rubescens*   **Mitrewort**   *Mitella breweri*

Grass-of-Parnassus   *Parnassia californica*

Five creamy white petals with greenish veins identify the blossoms of this showy plant. These inch-wide flowers are solitary, on the tops of 6- to 24-inch stems. Look carefully for the dainty fringed appendage (sterile stamen) at the base of each petal. The basal leaves are round or elliptic and 1 to 2 inches long. Grass-of-Parnassus frequents marshy places at moderate elevations and grows in the company of monkshood, bistort, and elephant's head. It is conspicuous in the damp swales around Grass Lake in the Desolation Wilderness of the Eldorado National Forest and along Whitney Creek in Sequoia National Park.

Found widely in northern and western North America.

Similar species: A closely related wildflower *(Parnassia fimbriata)* is found in boggy places in the northern Sierra. Its petals are fringed at the base, making it distinctive. It extends northward to Alaska.

Sierra Saxifrage   *Saxifraga aprica*

Sierra saxifrage grows on moist, stony soil from moderate elevations to subalpine and alpine areas. You can often see it in wet meadows near a melting snowbank. It has an overall purple color and is 3 to 8 inches tall. A few small, oblong or spatulate leaves adorn the base of the stem, and the flowers cluster tightly at the tip.

Found in the Sierra and Klamath Mountains north into southwestern Oregon and western Nevada.

Oregon Saxifrage   *Saxifraga oregana*

The saxifrage genus is widely distributed throughout the northern temperate zone. Oregon saxifrage, one of the more common and typical forms, grows from a stout rootstock and has a basal cluster of toothed, elliptic leaves, each from 1 to 5 inches long. The glandular stems, 1 to 2 feet tall, bear a loose cluster of white flowers at the tip.

Oregon saxifrage grows in boggy areas, along streams, and in wet meadows at mid and upper elevations. It is often almost lost to sight because it grows among taller grasses, sedges, and other lush vegetation.

Found in the Sierra Nevada north into Washington and Idaho.

Alpine Saxifrage   *Saxifraga tolmiei*

Alpine saxifrage nestles amid rock crannies and boulder fields. It is a low growing, mat-forming plant that provides a green border to the rock fields where it grows. The stems are trailing and somewhat woody. The rounded leaves, thick and succulent, crowd together on the stems. The flowering stems are only 2 to 3 inches tall and bear small, white-petaled flowers with purple-tipped stamens.

This little saxifrage is truly an alpine plant, growing mainly at timberline in rocky fell-fields, on scree slopes, and along rocky ridges, although it sometimes inhabits subalpine forest openings.

The specific name honors a pioneer surgeon and botanist, William Fraser Tolmie (1812–1886), who was stationed at the Hudson's Bay Company Fort Vancouver on the Columbia River.

Found in the Sierra Nevada north to Alaska.

Grass-of-Parnassus   *Parnassia californica*

Sierra Saxifrage   *Saxifraga aprica*

Oregon Saxifrage   *Saxifraga oregana*

Alpine Saxifrage   *Saxifraga tolmiei*

STONECROP FAMILY Crassulaceae

The stonecrop family consists of plants with thickened, succulent leaves. There are about fifteen hundred species of this family in the world; many have been cultivated and now adorn rock gardens. Hen-and-chickens, stonecrop, and live-forever are examples.

Stonecrop *Sedum obtusatum*

Stonecrops are notable for having succulent, alternate leaves. They absorb and store moisture when it is plentiful, releasing it to the plant during times of drought.

Most of the leaves of this stonecrop cluster in basal rosettes, which may form a mat of thick, succulent leaves. The leaves have blunt tips (referred to by the description *obtusatum*) and are somewhat reddish, especially toward the end of the growing season. The 2- to 6-inch-tall stems are often tinged with red and bear smaller oblong leaves. The yellow flowers fade to pale pink or cream late in the season.

This stonecrop grows in crevices or on otherwise smooth granite bluffs and ridges, from moderate elevations to timberline.

Found through the Sierra Nevada north into the southern Cascades.

Western Roseroot *Sedum rosea*

The several stems of this fleshy perennial emerge from a woody rootstock. Flat, sessile, oval leaves, about a half-inch in length, are distributed along the entire length of the 2- to 6-inch-tall stems, which are topped by a cluster of rose red or purple flowers. This stonecrop grows in moist, rocky places from the subalpine forest zone to above timberline. You'll find it blooming in July along cascading streams fed by snowmelt from higher elevations. Good places to look for it include the trail to Piute Pass in the Inyo National Forest and on Teneya Ridge within Yosemite National Park.

Found in the Sierra Nevada north to Alaska, east across northern North America, and in the northern Rockies.

Stonecrop   *Sedum obtusatum*   Western Roseroot   *Sedum rosea*

Stonecrop   *Sedum obtusatum*

SUNFLOWER FAMILY   Asteraceae

The sunflower family is a large, cosmopolitan group that contains more than twenty thousand species. It is the largest family of plants in California and is represented in every habitat in the state. This diverse group consists mainly of annuals and perennials. There are also a few shrubs or small trees represented.

The flowers are grouped into "heads," so that what appears as a single flower is actually a composite of many flowers. Basically, the flowers are of two types: flat, strap-shaped ones called rays and tubular ones called disks. The ray flowers consist of a flat, strap-shaped floret that looks like a single petal. Some flower heads—for instance, those of the dandelion—are composed entirely of ray-shaped flowers. Others—such as pearly everlasting—are composed of tubular flowers. Still other flower heads are composed of both types. The sunflower has tubular flowers in the central disk area and ray flowers along the margin. (See illustration in the glossary.)

Yarrow   *Achillea millefolium*

Yarrow, also called wild tansy and woolly yarrow, is a widely distributed plant. Recognize it by its fernlike leaves and white flower heads, composed of both disk and ray flowers. Growing 3 feet tall, the stems are densely covered with white, woolly hairs. Yarrow flourishes in a variety of situations and is at home in brushy areas, open woodlands, dry meadows, and roadsides. It immediately invades places where the natural vegetation has been disturbed. Yarrow has been used as a garden plant and can spread vigorously. A smaller form growing only 4 to 8 inches tall inhabits high-elevation alpine meadows and rocky fields.

Found through much of North America.

Orange Agoseris   *Agoseris aurantiaca*

The blossoms of orange agoseris resemble those of the common dandelion, but with orange flower heads rather than yellow. In the natural world of wildflowers orange is a rare color, making it stand out in a wildflower meadow. The flower heads of orange agoseris grow on slender, leafless stems that are up to 20 inches tall. Basal leaves are 2 to 10 inches long. When fresh, the flowers are a burnt orange; however, they sometimes turn purple or rose with age.

Orange agoseris grows in meadows and grassy openings at middle and upper elevations throughout the Sierra Nevada.

Found through most of the Sierra Nevada, north through the Cascade Range and east in the Rocky Mountains.

Yarrow *Achillea millefolium*   Yarrow growing in a dry setting
Achillea millefolium

Orange Agoseris *Agoseris aurantiaca*

Pearly Everlasting
Anaphalis margaritacea

Pearly everlasting is a bunched or loosely tufted perennial with 1- to 2-foot-tall stems and woolly white leaves. The flowers are in tight, round-topped clusters up to 6 inches across. The flower heads have yellow centers composed of tubular flowers. These heads are of two different types, female or seed-producing and male or pollen-producing. The flowers are surrounded by numerous overlapping rows of bracts that are pearly white, petal-like, and papery-textured. These last indefinitely—they seem "everlasting."

The name *margaritacea* means "pearly" and refers to the white color, which the common name also implies. When the flowers are young, the central yellow flowers are not very obvious. However, as the flower head matures, the white bracts spread, and the center flowers enlarge, becoming more conspicuous.

Pearly everlasting commonly grows in dense clumps on burned areas. The seeds are accompanied by a tuft of fine, straight hairs, allowing them to drift great distances with the wind. Once established, the creeping rootstocks aid the plant's rapid spread. Pearly everlasting grows mainly in open timber, on rocky flats and slopes, and in open meadows.

Found widely in North America, Europe, and Asia.

Rosy Everlasting
Antennaria rosea

Also called catsfoot and pussytoes, this is a perennial herb. The small flower heads sit atop 2- to 10-inch-tall stems that are covered with dense, woolly hairs and have narrow, alternate leaves. Additional spoon- or wedge-shaped leaves are clumped at the base of the stems. In everlastings, the bracts are the most conspicuous part of the flower head, being white, brown, pink, or rose. This everlasting is distinguished by the rose-colored bracts at the base of each flower head.

Rosy everlasting commonly grows in woolly mats or tufts, sometimes covering several square feet of ground. It resides at middle and upper elevations in a variety of habitats, including open, dry sites, moist meadows, alpine rock fields, and open woodlands.

Found widely in the mountains of western North America.

Similar species: Two additional species are worth mentioning. *Antennaria corymbosa* inhabits mid-elevation moist meadows. Its slender stems grow about 6 inches tall, and horizontal stolons form loose mats. The basal leaves are spoon-shaped, and the bracts beneath the flower heads are pale, with black or dark brown near the base. *A. media* grows at upper elevations in alpine meadows and ridges. Its many stolons form dense mats. The upper portion of the bracts are dark brown.

Pearly Everlasting   *Anaphalis margaritacea*

Rosy Everlasting   *Antennaria rosea*   *Antennaria media*

Heartleaf Arnica
Arnica cordifolia

Heartleaf arnica is a delightful little wildflower, growing in shaded woodlands and, occasionally, amid the grasses of forest openings. The bright yellow flower heads are sometimes more than 2 inches across. The erect, somewhat sticky stems are 8 to 24 inches tall (although dwarf varieties are sometimes found) and have two to four pairs of opposite leaves, the lower ones being distinctly heart-shaped. The descriptive name *cordifolia* is derived from the Latin words meaning "heart" and "leaf." The genus is named for the medicinal arnica, a popular remedy for bruises, sprains, and other soreness, and obtained from the flower and rootstocks of a European species of this genus.

Of some ten kinds of arnica found in the Sierra, heartleaf arnica is probably the most common. Other arnicas are distinguished by differences in leaf arrangement and shape and in the floral head. Arnicas are sometimes mistaken for groundsels (see page 184) because they also have yellow sunflower-like heads. However, arnica leaves are opposite each other, while those of groundsels are alternately arranged on the stem.

Found in the mountains of western North America.

Big Sagebrush
Artemisia tridentata

Big sagebrush is a particularly common shrub on the eastern slopes of the Sierra and is widespread throughout the Great Basin. It is an aromatic shrub, especially after a rain or when its leaves have been crushed. It is a many-branched shrub that normally grows 3 to 4 feet tall, although under certain conditions it may grow up to 8 or 9 feet tall. Distinguish this species of sagebrush by its leaves, which are about 1 inch long and divided into three lobes, as described by the name *tridentata*. The small flowers form elongated clusters and bloom in late summer and early fall.

Found in the western and central United States, east of the Sierra-Cascade divide.

Alpine Aster
Aster alpigenus

Also known as dwarf purple aster, this little flower is common in high mountain meadows and alpine boulder fields, where it dots moist openings. The structure of its leaves and stems give it an identifying characteristic. Its narrow, often grasslike, deep green leaves are mostly basal, from 2 to 6 inches long, and tapered at the base. The 2- to 16-inch-tall stem, however, is horizontal before becoming erect, appearing to arise from the side of the basal cluster of leaves. The floral heads have yellow centers and pink or purple ray flowers. This aster commonly grows in small colonies, thus covering an extensive area.

Found in the mountains of the Pacific states.

Heartleaf Arnica   *Arnica cordifolia*   **Big Sagebrush**   *Artemisia tridentata*

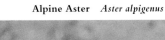

Alpine Aster   *Aster alpigenus*

Western Mountain Aster
Aster occidentalis

Western aster adorns the borders of drying meadows and ponds or shaded forest edges, blooming in August and into September when other wildflowers have faded and the grasses and sedges have dried and turned brown. The stems are 8 to 20 inches tall and have oblanceolate leaves along their entire length. The flower heads contain violet or lavender ray flowers and yellow disk flowers. These showy heads are 1 to 2 inches wide. Western mountain aster grows at moderate elevations in the Sierra Nevada at such spots as Iceberg Meadows in the Eldorado National Forest and Crane Flat in Yosemite National Park.

Asters are sometimes confused with the fleabanes, also members of the sunflower family. Generally speaking, fleabanes bloom early in the summer while asters bloom later in the summer and fall. However, this is not a good criterion to use because mountain summers are usually short and summer quickly merges into fall, especially at higher elevations. The ray flowers of fleabanes are usually more numerous and narrower than those of asters. Once you recognize several individuals, this characteristic should help you distinguish the two groups.

Found through the mountain ranges of western North America.

Similar species: Long-leaved aster *(Aster ascendens)* grows on the eastern slopes of the Sierra Nevada. Its slender stems usually grow from 8 to 30 inches tall and have linear leaves in the middle and oblanceolate leaves at the base. It, too, has violet ray flowers and yellow or gold disk flowers. A good place to look for it is on the trail to Glen Alpine in the Desolation Wilderness.

Balsam-Root
Balsamorhiza sagittata

Balsam-root's bright yellow flowers herald spring in the mountains. The flower heads are usually solitary on a 1- to 2-foot-long stem. The large basal leaves are 4 to 12 inches long, triangular or arrowhead-shaped, and covered with white, woolly hairs, especially on the undersides. This gives a slightly whitish tinge to the leaves, especially early in the season.

Balsam-root grows at mid-elevations on dry, well-drained slopes or in open pine forests, often in the company of sagebrush and scrub pine.

The name *balsam-root* refers to the thick taproot, which Native Americans used for food. *Sagittata* refers to the arrowhead-like leaf shape.

Found in much of the Sierra Nevada north along the eastern slopes of the Cascades into Canada and east into the Rocky Mountains.

Western Mountain Aster   *Aster occidentalis*

Balsam-Root   *Balsamorhiza sagittata*

Rubber Rabbitbrush   *Chrysothamnus nauseosus*

The cone-shaped, bright buttery yellow flower heads of this shrub are located around the periphery of the plant, giving it a golden glow or halo. When not in bloom, rabbitbrush is identified by its alternate, linear leaves, which are covered by fine, feltlike hairs, especially on the young outer stems. The result is an overall white or gray tinge. This species grows 1 to 7 feet tall.

Rubber rabbitbrush is a late bloomer, flowering from August through October. It grows on dry, open plains and mountain slopes, often associated with big sagebrush and Jeffrey pine. You will also see it in waste areas or disturbed sites, such as along roadways.

Found widely in the drier areas of western North America.

Anderson Thistle   *Cirsium andersonii*

Thistles are not usually thought of as being beautiful wildflowers. Instead, we tend to think of them as weeds that invade open pastures and meadows. Their prickly leaves are rough and sharp, further degrading them in many people's eyes. However, most thistles are quite pretty. Anderson thistle is one of the most attractive to grace our mountain roadsides. Its purple stem grows 1 to 4 feet tall and has leaves with spiny lobes and teeth.

The showy blossoms appear from July to September at moderate and upper elevations in the Sierra. It grows in meadows and on open slopes.

Found in the Sierra Nevada north into Idaho.

Elk Thistle   *Cirsium scariosum*

Elk thistle is an attractive plant with short stems and mostly spiny leaves that are 4 to 12 inches long. The leaves are either basal or tightly packed on a short stem. Tufts of cream, yellow, or pale purple flowers are tucked in a rosette of basal leaves or clustered on the tips of the short, leafy stems. The plants may grow close to the ground and only about 12 inches tall or have short stems up to 2 feet tall.

Found in the Sierra Nevada north into British Columbia and in much of the Rocky Mountains.

Orange Sneezeweed   *Dugaldia hoopesii*

Orange sneezeweed grows 10 to 30 inches tall and has a leafy stem with oblong leaves. Both the ray and disk flowers are burnt orange or yellow, with the floral head reaching 2 to 3 inches across. Orange sneezeweed begins blooming in early July at the edge of melting snowbanks. You'll find it in damp, well-drained slopes in the company of aspen, in parklands amid ponderosa pine, fir, and spruce, or in moist meadows up to timberline. In August it may still be blooming in the same area but in places where the snow lingered longer. A good place to spot it is along Sonora Pass.

Found in the central and southern Sierra Nevada and east into the Rocky Mountains.

Rubber Rabbitbrush   *Chrysothamnus nauseosus*

Anderson Thistle   *Cirsium andersonii*

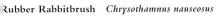

Elk Thistle   *Cirsium scariosum*

Orange Sneezeweed   *Dugaldia hoopesii*

Bloomer Goldenbush
Ericameria bloomeri

A compact, woody shrub that blooms late in the summer, bloomer goldenbush sometimes lines Sierra Nevada roadways, utilizing the water running off the highway and producing a luxurious, low-growing hedge. The yellow flower heads cluster at the tips of the branches and have one to five ray flowers and up to twelve disk flowers (occasionally, the flower heads have only disk flowers). The branches grow up to 2 feet tall and bear narrow, linear leaves.

This goldenbush inhabits dry, open places, from middle elevations up to timberline.

Found through the Sierra Nevada north into Washington and east into Nevada.

Cut-Leaved Daisy
Erigeron compositus

This compact little fleabane is known by its leaves, which are divided or cut along their tips. Only those who are willing to hike into high alpine areas will find these flowers, tucked into the safety of rocky crevices. The leaves crowd onto short, thick stalks that are only a few inches tall. The nearly inch-wide flower heads, with pale purple or nearly white ray flowers and yellow disk flowers, cover the leafy mat.

Most Sierran fleabanes have flower heads with both ray and disk flowers. The tubular center disk flowers are usually yellow; the numerous petal-like ray flowers are pink, purple, or white. All the alpine species described here grow from stout taproots.

Found from the Sierra Nevada north to Alaska and east across North America; also in the Rocky Mountains.

Similar species: Several other fleabanes may be encountered in the high country. Another inhabitant of rocky areas, *Erigeron vagus* grows about 2 inches tall and has similar flowers. The spoon-shaped leaves, however, are divided into three lobes. **Dwarf daisy** *(E. pygmaeus)* and **Sierra daisy** *(E. algidus)* also dwell in rocky places near timberline. However, their leaves are entire, instead of being cut or divided. Their flower heads have blue or purple ray flowers. Dwarf daisy is a compact plant with mostly basal leaves and barely grows 2 inches tall. It is found in the central Sierra and adjacent Nevada. Sierra daisy grows a little taller, up to 10 inches high. Although most of the egg-shaped leaves are clustered at the base, a few narrow leaves may also be found along the flowering stems. This fleabane is found in alpine areas from Mount Whitney to Lake Tahoe.

Bloomer Goldenbush   *Ericameria bloomeri*

Cut-Leaved Daisy   *Erigeron compositus*

Dwarf Daisy   *Erigeron pygmaeus*

Aster Fleabane

Erigeron peregrinus

Many mountain travelers regard aster fleabane, also called wandering daisy, as the most showy and common fleabane of the higher mountains. It has stems up to 30 inches tall, although most are from 12 to 24 inches tall. The lower portion of the stem is quite leafy, with clumps of oblong leaves 3 to 8 inches long. The flower heads are 1 inch or more across and have violet or purple ray flowers and yellow disk flowers.

Aster fleabane commonly inhabits moderate and upper elevations, where it grows in moist meadows and alongside meandering streams. You will find it blooming along the headwaters of the Tuolumne River and in the moist meadows adjacent to Tioga Pass Road in Yosemite National Park in July and August.

Found throughout the mountains of western North America.

Similar species: Several other showy fleabanes are found at moderate and lower elevations in the Sierra Nevada. **Daisy fleabane *(Erigeron strigosus)*** has smaller flower heads that are less than 1 inch wide. The numerous ray flowers are white or pale purple. The stems are 10 to 30 inches tall, branch at the top, and have 2- to 4-inch bristly leaves. This fleabane is not native to California but was introduced from the eastern United States. It grows in moist meadows at moderate and lower elevations and blooms from June to early August.

Brewer daisy *(E. breweri)* and **leafy daisy *(E. foliosus)*** both inhabit drier places. They have blue or purple ray flowers and yellow disk flowers. Brewer daisy has erect or trailing stems 4 to 12 inches long. The leaves are oblong or rounded, about 1 inch long, and have stiff hairs. It grows in rocky areas from 5,000 to 10,500 feet elevation. Leafy daisy grows on grassy hillsides or dry slopes, usually below 6,000 feet elevation. Its stems grow 1 or 2 feet tall and have narrow, linear leaves 1 or 2 inches long. The flower heads are about 1 inch in diameter.

Woolly Sunflower

Eriophyllum lanatum

Also known as golden yarrow, this delightful little yellow sunflower brightens dry roadsides and rocky bluffs. A highly variable species, it exists in many forms. At upper elevations in the Sierra it is a shrubby, compact plant, usually about 5 to 11 inches tall. At middle elevations its slender stems have a more open form. White, woolly hairs cover the leaves and stems. Both the names *Eriophyllum* and *lanatum* mean "hairy" and refer to this trait. The leaves are often so toothed or lobed that their shape would best be called irregular. Both the ray flowers and disk flowers are a vivid, golden yellow on flower heads one-half inch across.

Found in the Sierra Nevada north to British Columbia and also in the Rocky Mountains.

Aster Fleabane *Erigeron peregrinus*

Leafy Daisy *Erigeron foliosus*   **Woolly Sunflower** *Eriophyllum lanatum*

Bigelow Sneezeweed
Helenium bigelovii

This sneezeweed is an attractive and common component of mid-elevation Sierran meadows. Standing 2 to 3 feet tall, its dome-shaped flower heads are easy to recognize. The golden brown disk flowers are surrounded by drooping yellow or bronze rays. Lance-shaped, sessile leaves, 4 to 10 inches long and about 1 inch wide, clasp the stem.

Bigelow sneezeweed grows in moist meadows, marshy spots, and along stream banks. Places to look for it include Quaking Aspen Meadow in the Sequoia National Forest and Crane Flat in Yosemite National Park.

Found throughout the Sierra Nevada north into the Coast Ranges of California and into Oregon.

White Hawkweed
Hieracium albiflorum

This little hawkweed, typified by its small (an eighth-inch wide) flower heads atop slender 8- to 30-inch-tall stems, grows throughout the Sierra. It is common and widespread, thriving in the partial shade of dry, coniferous forests. The flower heads are composed of creamy white ray flowers, each ray being squared at the tip. The leaves are mostly basal, although a few may be scattered along the stem. Long, white hairs cover the lance-shaped or oblong leaves.

The name *Hieracium* is derived from the Greek word for "hawk," resulting in the common name. According to ancient legend, hawks used the sap of these plants to improve their eyesight—although the legend neglects to say how the predaceous birds utilized the plant material! The specific name is derived from the Latin *albus,* "white," and *flos,* "flower," referring to the white flowers.

Found widely in western North America.

Shaggy Hawkweed
Hieracium horridum

Shaggy leaves, densely covered with long brown or whitish hairs, identify this hawkweed. Nestled in granite crevices and on rocky slopes, the flowers are hardly noticed among the 3- to 4-inch-long leaves. The branching stems, from 4 to 15 inches high, bear small, bright yellow flowers that bloom in July and August. You'll find this common Sierra wildflower on dry, open rocky areas, from the montane forest to timberline.

Found in the mountains of southern California in the Sierra Nevada north into Oregon.

Bigelow Sneezeweed   *Helenium bigelovii*   **White Hawkweed**   *Hieracium albiflorum*

Shaggy Hawkweed   *Hieracium horridum*

Alpine Gold
Hulsea algida

Also called alpine sunflower, this is truly a plant of high, windy places. Rarely found below 10,000 feet elevation, alpine gold makes its home on open exposed ridges and rocky swales. It rivals sky pilot (see page 126) as a reward for hikers who trek into the high country for alpine vistas. Growing 4 to 16 inches tall, alpine gold has golden flower heads that are 1 to 2 inches wide and bloom from July through August. The basal leaves are oblong and irregularly toothed. More noticeable, however, is their soft, sticky feel and strong odor.

Although not abundant, alpine gold is locally common in many alpine places, such as the slopes of Mount Dana within Yosemite National Park or Mount Rose in the Tahoe basin. Often alpine gold's upright posture and golden color, so characteristic and vivid when the flower blooms first appear, become battered by midsummer storms.

Found on the high peaks of the Sierra Nevada, north into Oregon, Nevada, and Montana.

Similar species: Another Sierra hulsea, **pumice hulsea** *(Hulsea vestita),* grows in open, sandy places at lower elevations. A variable species, it ranges from the sagebrush flats to timberline of the southern Sierra Nevada. It stands 12 inches tall and has woolly white leaves clustered at the base. Each stem bears a single yellow flower head that may be tinged with purple. A dwarf form only 2 inches tall grows at timberline.

Sierra Lessingia
Lessingia leptoclada

Creating a sea of pale purple or lavender, Sierra lessingia thrives in dry openings within the lower-elevation pine forests. The lavender flower heads are composed entirely of tubular flowers. However, the outer flowers have palmate petals, giving the appearance of ray-shaped flowers. The branching stems grow up to 2 feet tall. A heavy rainstorm in midsummer can leave the flower heads and stems looking battered and ragged, but they resume their perky appearance after drying in the sun. Look for Sierra lessingia in the Indian Basin area of the Sequoia National Forest or on the floor of Yosemite Valley in early August.

Found in open meadows through most of the Sierra Nevada.

Common Madia
Madia elegans

A common wildflower on open, dry slopes in the foothills and at moderate elevations in the Sierra Nevada, common madia resembles a wild sunflower. The plants grow up to 30 inches tall and bear several flower heads. These showy heads are nearly 2 inches wide, with yellow tubular flowers in the central disk and yellow ray flowers. Sometimes there is a maroon or brown spot on each ray flower, making each head quite elegant. Often you will see this madia blooming along the roadsides in the morning, but by noon you will be hard pressed to find the showy flower heads. This is because most of them close by midmorning, the tips of the ray flowers curling inward. By late afternoon, they reopen.

Tarweed, the common name for this group of wildflowers, refers to sticky stems and leaves.

Found widely in the grasslands and slopes at lower elevations in the Sierra Nevada, north into Oregon and into the Great Basin.

Alpine Gold   *Hulsea algida*   **Sierra Lessingia**   *Lessingia leptoclada*

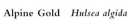

Common Madia   *Madia elegans*

Nodding Microseris   *Microseris nutans*

A yellow-flowered plant growing about 12 inches tall, this wildflower reminds one of a slender dandelion. Like that of the common weed that invades many lowland gardens, the flower head is composed of yellow ray flowers and lacks disk flowers. The flower heads nod before they bloom, giving rise to the common name. Nodding microseris has linear or lance-shaped leaves on the lower part of the stem that are 4 to 10 inches long and either entire or toothed. The flower heads are yellow.

This is a common and widespread species in the Sierra Nevada. It grows along forest and meadow borders at moderate and upper elevations.

Found from California north into British Columbia, east into the Rocky Mountains.

Alpine Dandelion   *Nothocalais alpestris*

Alpine dandelion resembles the common plant of yards and gardens. It has narrow, basal leaves with slightly toothed edges. The stems have a milky sap, stand 6 to 10 inches tall, and bear a solitary yellow flower head of ray-shaped flowers. Alpine dandelion grows in moist meadows at upper elevations in the northern Sierra Nevada.

Found from the northern Sierra Nevada into the Cascades to Washington.

Golden-Aster   *Pyrrocoma apargoides*

Golden-aster is 10 to 15 inches tall, has toothed basal leaves 1 to 4 inches long, and has solitary yellow flower heads. A single flower head adorns each stem. The stems are usually decumbent, meaning they lie on the ground, although they may sometimes stand semierect. The general effect is of stems matted down on each other. The leaves are basal, linear, and somewhat leathery. Golden-aster inhabits dry meadows and other open areas at higher elevations and timberline, blooming from July through September.

Found through the Sierra Nevada and east into Nevada.

Silver Raillardella   *Raillardella argentea*

Growing on open slopes of granite and on pumice ridges, silver raillardella is a small plant, less than 4 inches tall. A single flower head of orange disk flowers sits atop the short, leafless stem; the leaves are basal and are covered with soft, silvery hairs. Silver raillardella commonly grows in colonies that cover a large area with these soft, silvery leaves, which identify the plant even when it is not in bloom.

The flowers appear in July and August, depending on elevation and exposure, and are locally common above timberline. Look for them while hiking in the vicinity of the Hall Natural Area in the Inyo National Forest or Castle Pass in the Tahoe National Forest. Finding a colony of this attractive wildflower is ample reward for climbing and hiking at higher elevations.

Found in the Sierra Nevada north into the Cascades of Oregon.

Nodding Microseris   *Microseris nutans*   **Alpine Dandelion**   *Nothocalais alpestris*

Golden-Aster   *Pyrrocoma apargoides*   **Silver Raillardella**   *Raillardella argentea*

Sierran Raillardella   *Raillardella scaposa*

Often growing near silver raillardella, Sierra raillardella is similar but lacks the covering of silvery hairs. Its green leaves are mostly basal, and the leafless stems are between 2 and 16 inches tall. Although the flower head usually consists entirely of disk flowers, occasionally ray flowers are also present. This raillardella grows in dry rocky or gravelly areas and along dry meadow borders from moderate elevations to timberline.

Found in the Sierra Nevada of California, the Oregon Cascades, and western Nevada.

Coneflower   *Rudbeckia californica*

Coneflower is an appropriate name for this easily recognized wildflower of mid-elevation openings. The flower heads are cone-shaped, usually solitary, with the brown tubular flowers elevated above the yellow ray flowers. An erect, leafy plant 2 to 4 feet tall, coneflower has rough, hairy leaves that are 2 to 4 inches long. Widely scattered throughout the Sierra, coneflower is rarely abundant in any one place. However, you might look for it at Eagle Lakes in the Tahoe National Forest and in Kings Canyon.

Found through much of the Sierra Nevada north into Oregon.

Black-Eyed Susan   *Rudbeckia hirta*

Black-eyed Susan inhabits places similar to those where coneflower grows, and the two plants commonly grow together. Usually several flower heads form near the top of the 2- to 4-foot-tall stems. The ray flowers are orange or yellow, and the disk flowers are a rich brown. Black-eyed Susan was originally native to the eastern states and is the state flower of Maryland. Introduced into many areas of the western United States by early settlers, it is now common along roadsides and in dry meadows, where it blooms in July and August.

Found through much of North America.

Single-Stemmed Groundsel   *Senecio integerrimus*

Known as groundsels, ragworts, and butterweeds, the *Senecio* genus is extremely large, with some forty species growing in California alone. The name *Senecio* comes from the Latin *senex,* meaning "old man," and probably refers to the white hairs on the seeds. You can usually recognize groundsels by a series of characteristics. The bracts below the flower head are in a single row. The leaves are arranged alternately on the stems, although in a few species they are mostly basal. Groundsels could be confused with some species of arnica because both have yellow sunflower-like heads. However, arnicas have stem leaves that are opposite each other, not alternate.

Single-stemmed groundsel is a common forest component that dwells in the partial shade of ponderosa pine and lodgepole pine forests, from foothill areas to timberline. This stout-stemmed plant grows from 1 to 3 feet tall. Most of the leaves cluster at the bottom of the stem, being greatly reduced in size on the stem itself. The flower heads, about 1 inch wide, have both ray and tubular flowers. They bloom from May through August, depending on elevation.

Found through the Sierra Nevada and the northern coastal mountains, north into Oregon.

Sierran Raillardella *Raillardella scaposa*

Coneflower *Rudbeckia californica*

Black-Eyed Susan *Rudbeckia hirta*

Single-Stemmed Groundsel *Senecio integerrimus*

Arrowleaf Butterweed
Senecio triangularis

Patches of arrowleaf butterweed lend vivid color to a landscape—and indicate a moist slope or seep. The leafy stems of this robust plant may grow as tall as 6 feet, although 3-foot plants are more common. Both the specific name and part of the common name allude to the arrowlike shape of the leaves. The name *butterweed* refers to the yellow flower heads. Although ranging from moderate elevations to timberline, butterweed grows best in cool, higher elevations, where it often forms extensive patches. There it blooms from mid-July through August.

Found widely in the mountains of western North America.

Similar species: Clark groundsel *(Senecio clarkianus)* also inhabits moist sites, especially mid-elevation meadows, and blooms in July and August. It is found in the central and southern Sierra and grows 2 to 4 feet tall. The 2- to 8-inch-long leaves are lance-shaped or oblong, not triangular, and have deeply cut leaf margins. **S. pauciflorus** blooms in July and August in subalpine or alpine meadows. It has thick, basal leaves and orange flower heads that usually lack ray flowers.

Creek Goldenrod
Solidago canadensis

Also known as meadow goldenrod, this wildflower grows 2 or 3 feet tall along stream banks and meadow borders, especially where the ground is moist. The pyramidal spray of yellow flowers appears in July or August, continuing to bloom through the fall. Many goldenrods are difficult to tell apart, but as a group their many constant features make them fairly easy to recognize. They are perennial herbs with alternate, mostly toothed leaves and erect heads of yellow flowers. Each head is surrounded by several series of overlapping bracts.

The flowers of some species have been used to make a yellow dye, lending color to Native American crafts and clothing. The leaves are also reported to have been boiled to make a preparation for cuts and other wounds. The genus name comes from the Latin word meaning "to make whole."

Found widely in North America.

Similar species: Alpine goldenrod *(S. multiradiata)* grows above 8,000 feet elevation and rarely exceeds 12 inches in height. It has lance-shaped, mostly entire leaves, with basal leaves that are larger than those on the stem. Common in high-elevation meadows, it is found throughout the Sierra and also in the Rocky Mountains and Cascade Range.

Whitneya
Whitneya dealbata

Whitneya is another member of the sunflower family with yellow flower heads and opposite leaves that could be confused with the arnicas (see page 168). However, the leaves of whitneya are covered with fine hairs, giving them a silver color. It grows 10 to 20 inches tall and has flower heads 2 to 3 inches across. This showy flower is not especially common, but look for it in dry openings within the montane and subalpine forest.

Whitneya, endemic to California, was named for the pioneer geologist Josiah Whitney (1819–96) of the California Geological Survey. The 14,495-foot Mount Whitney also bears his name.

Found in the central and northern Sierra Nevada.

Arrowleaf Butterweed *Senecio triangularis*

Creek Goldenrod *Solidago canadensis*

Alpine Goldenrod *Solidago multiradiata*

Whitneya *Whitneya dealbata*

Woolly Mule Ears   *Wyethia mollis*

The bright yellow flowers of mule ears, sometimes called wild sunflower, dot dry slopes and hillsides above 5,000 feet, especially on the eastern slopes of the Sierra Nevada. Often they mingle with sagebrush and scrub pine. The flower heads, usually solitary at the ends of the 1- to 3-foot-tall stems, may be as large as 3 inches across. The oblong leaves, 7 to 19 inches long and 2 to 7 inches wide, are clumped at the base of the plant. Smaller leaves, usually less than 5 inches long, occur alternately on the flowering stem. The leaves, especially when young, are covered with soft, white hairs, which give them a silvery appearance and inspire the common name.

The genus name honors Captain Nathaniel Wyeth, early American trapper and traveler, who crossed North America in 1834. He collected *Wyethia,* and the genus was named for him.

Found in the central and northern Sierra to southeastern Oregon and in the Great Basin and northern Rocky Mountains.

Similar species: Narrow-leaved mule ears *(Wyethia angustifolia)* has narrower leaves (about 3 inches wide) that lack a woolly covering. This mule ears, about 2 feet tall, grows on open slopes at lower elevations. Where both species occur, look at the flower heads. Few ray flowers adorn each woolly mule ears, while narrow-leaved mule ears has many (usually more than ten) ray flowers.

SWEET-SHRUB FAMILY   Calycanthaceae

This is a small family of perhaps six species. They are all shrubs, some evergreen, some deciduous, but all aromatic. Two species grow in the United States, one in California.

Spicebush   *Calycanthus occidentalis*

Also known as sweetbush, this delightful shrub grows from the foothills to moderate elevations in the mountains. You can easily recognize it by its glossy green leaves and the rust red or rose-colored flowers that bloom from April to August. The common name *spicebush* comes mainly from the fragrant odor of the leaves, especially strong when bruised or crushed. Spicebush prefers fairly moist places, such as canyon bottoms and stream and lake margins. You may see it along the Merced River at the Arch Rock entrance to Yosemite National Park.

Sometimes it is difficult to distinguish between a bush or shrub and a small tree. Technically, a shrub is a woody plant, usually with smaller proportions than a tree, but with several branches coming from the base rather than one main trunk.

This is the only species of *Calycanthus* found in western North America; another species of this genus grows in the southeastern United States. Indeed, the descriptive name *occidentalis* means "western" and indicates the location of this species.

Found in the Coast Range and western Sierra Nevada.

Woolly Mule Ears   *Wyethia mollis*

Spicebush   *Calycanthus occidentalis*

VIOLET FAMILY   Violaceae

The violet family contains some six hundred species of plants and is one of the better-known groups of wildflowers in the world. Violets are largely herbaceous plants with basal or alternate leaves. The flowers are showy, with five petals arranged in a characteristic pattern: two upper petals, two lateral petals, and a larger, lower petal that extends backward to form a shallow sac or spur at its base. Nearly every English-speaking country in the world has and loves its native violets. A few cultivated members of this family, for instance the pansy, adorn our finest gardens.

Western Long-Spurred Violet   *Viola adunca*

In the western long-spurred violet the spur of the fifth petal (see family description) is very pronounced, being almost as long as the remainder of the flower. The flowers are a deep violet or pale blue, although a few white specimens are occasionally seen. The flowers are a half-inch to 1 inch long. The plants grow 2 to 5 inches tall and have round or oval leaves that are 1 to 2 inches long.

Western long-spurred violet can be found in a variety of habitats. It grows on grassy slopes, at the edges of meadows, and in the partial shade at the edge of forest openings.

Found widely in the mountainous regions of western North America, east across the continent to eastern North America.

Stream Violet   *Viola glabella*

About twenty species of violet grow in California. Only about a fourth of these are blue; most are yellow, white, or purple. Stream violet is a yellow-flowered species that grows up to 12 inches tall. The erect stems sprout from a scaly rhizome. Stream violet has bright green, basal, heart-shaped leaves. The lower petal of this showy violet has three purple veins, while the lateral petals are bearded at the throat.

Stream violet grows not only along wet stream banks but also in shaded, damp areas such as forest edges. It ranges from lower elevations to moderate elevations in the Sierra Nevada.

Found widely in the Pacific states, east into Montana.

Similar species: Several other yellow-flowered species bloom in the Sierra. One is **mountain violet (*Viola purpurea*),** which grows throughout the open conifer forests. Less than 8 inches tall, this violet has spreading, egg-shaped leaves that are slightly toothed along the edges. They are often tinged with purple. The upper flower petals are also brown- or purple-tinged on their undersides.

Two species of violet with lobed leaves are **Shelton's violet (*V. sheltonii*)** and **pine violet (*V. lobata*).** Pine violet is 3 to 20 inches tall and has leaves divided into three to nine fingerlike, irregular segments. The flowers are yellow, with all or at least the lower petals lined with purple at their base. Shelton's violet also has divided leaves. They have three lobes that are further subdivided. The flowers have five yellow petals; the lower petal has three brownish veins, the lateral petals are bearded, and the two upper ones are backed with brown.

Western Long-Spurred Violet *Viola adunca*

Stream Violet *Viola glabella*

Mountain Violet *Viola purpurea*

Macloskey's Violet   *Viola macloskeyi*

Macloskey's violet is a dainty little plant that grows 3 to 6 inches tall from an underground rhizome. Spreading by runners over the ground, it may form a small colony. The flower petals are white, sometimes with three purple veins on the lower petal. Macloskey's violet grows in moist, boggy sites such as the edge of marshes that are fed by run-off from melting snow.

Found in northern and central California north into Canada and east across northern North America.

WATERLEAF FAMILY   Hydrophyllaceae

The waterleaf family contains annuals, perennials, and some small shrubs. They are generally hairy and are widely found in western North America. The family usually has small flowers that collectively may be quite showy. The flowers form cymes, branched floral groups where the central or uppermost flower blooms before those on the edge. In some genera the cymes are coiled. The floral parts are usually in fives. The waterleaf genera, except for draperia, have some (or all) of their leaves alternate along the stem or clustered at the base. Phacelias, which belong to this family, are often cultivated for garden use.

Draperia   *Draperia systyla*

Draperia, the only species in this genus, is a low, spreading plant, often covering several feet with a loose mat. The paired leaves are 1 to 2 inches long and covered with soft, silky hairs. The pale purple, tubular flowers are about a quarter-inch long on a coiled stem. The coiled floral stems are typical of the borage and waterleaf families (additional characters divide these groups). Draperia is the only perennial member of the waterleaf family with all its leaves in pairs. Draperia grows on dry slopes within Sierra Nevada forests, from the foothills up to about 8,000 feet.

Found through the Sierra Nevada into northern California.

Fivespot   *Nemophilia maculata*

A bank decorated with these annuals is a sure sign of spring. They bloom from April to July, from the foothills up to 7,500 feet elevation. The spreading stems are 3 to 12 inches long and have opposite leaves. The lower leaves are deeply lobed, the upper ones entire. The flower is saucer-shaped, up to 1 or 2 inches across. The clean, white flowers have one large, purple spot at the tip of each petal.

Fivespot is abundant in the Sierra foothills, where it prefers moist, open meadows and slopes, hollows, road banks, and woodlands. Look for it along the road to Mineral King in Sequoia National Park or along the Hetch Hetchy Road in Yosemite National Park.

Found in the Sierra and Central Valley of California.

Similar species: Sierra nemophilia *(Nemophila spatulata)* somewhat resembles fivespot. The white or blue flowers, although much smaller, are often dotted and sometimes have purple blotches on the floral lobes. Its weak, usually sprawling, stems are 4 to 12 inches long. It ranges from 4,000 to 10,500 feet elevation throughout the Sierra.

Macloskey's Violet *Viola macloskeyi*

Draperia *Draperia systyla*

Fivespot *Nemophilia maculata*

Baby Blue-Eyes   *Nemophila menziesii*

Baby blue-eyes rivals fivespot for our attention in the Sierra foothills during the spring. Its sprawling stems are about 12 inches long and have opposite leaves, the upper ones being nearly sessile. The five pale or bright blue petals form a saucer-shaped flower with a light center. However, the flower color varies, sometimes being an overall pale blue. Common in the foothills, baby blue-eyes can be found in May along the Foresta Road in Yosemite National Park.

Baby blue-eyes is easily started from seed and makes a colorful addition to any wildflower garden, creating a blue hue over the ground.

Found along the western slopes of the Sierra Nevada.

Timberline Phacelia   *Phacelia hastata*

The phacelias are a large and varied group, with nearly ninety species represented in California alone. They are herbaceous plants, and most have bluish or white flowers. The flowers are densely coiled in spikes reminiscent of a fiddlehead. This book treats only a few of the more widespread species.

Tucked amid rocky crevices and slopes, timberline phacelia rarely grows more than 10 inches tall. Its foliage appears gray, being covered with stiff hairs. The lance-shaped leaves are entire, not lobed or separated as in many other phacelias. The pale lavender or almost white flowers coil tightly in spikes reminiscent of a violin fiddlehead. The coiled flower cluster is typical of phacelias. Timberline phacelia grows above 7,000 feet elevation and can be found on most high Sierra passes and plateaus above timberline. It blooms from July through September.

Found through the Sierra Nevada north into southern Oregon.

Waterleaf Phacelia   *Phacelia hydrophylloides*

Nestled on the floor of red fir and ponderosa pine forests, waterleaf phacelia has 12-inch-long stems that spread over the ground or, occasionally, are erect. The silky leaves are distributed over the entire length of the stem and are generally ovate or oblong in shape. The lower leaves are deeply lobed, while the upper leaves are merely toothed. Pale violet or white bell-shaped flowers form dense, terminal clusters, the extended stamens giving a fringed appearance.

Found in the Sierra Nevada north into Washington and east into Nevada.

Similar species: Caterpillar plant (*Phacelia mutabilis*) has flowers of varying color (*mutabilis* means "varied"), ranging from pale green or white to lavender. The flowers are less than a half-inch long and crowded onto a dense coil, resulting in the common name. The plants are from 8 to 20 inches tall, and most of the leaves are basal. These tufted lower leaves are lanceolate or ovate and may have one or two pairs of lateral leaflets. Both fine and coarse hairs cover the entire plant. This phacelia is common in light shade and rocky zones at mid-elevations through most of the Sierra Nevada.

Baby Blue-Eyes *Nemophilia menziesii*   **Timberline Phacelia** *Phacelia hastata*

Waterleaf Phacelia *Phacelia hydrophylloides*

Identifying Sierra Nevada Conifers

Pines: needles in bundles or clusters, usually held together by a thin sheath; woody cones with thick scales

Whitebark pine *(Pinus albicaulis)*
five needles per bundle
cone scale without prickles
near timberline

Foxtail pine *(Pinus balfouriana)*
five needles per bundle
cone scale with small, incurved prickle
upper elevations on dry, rocky slopes

Western white pine *(Pinus monticola)*
five needles per bundle
cones slender, 4 to 10 inches long
red fir/lodgepole pine forest

Sugar pine *(Pinus lambertiana)*
five needles per bundle
cones slender, 10 to 20 inches long
mixed conifer forest

Ponderosa pine *(Pinus ponderosa)*
three needles per bundle
cones 6 to 12 inches long
cone scale turned outward
mixed conifer forest

Jeffrey pine *(Pinus jeffreyi)*
three needles per bundle
cones 6 to 12 inches long
cone scale turned inward
dry rocky slopes on montane forest, especially on eastern side
   of Sierra Nevada

Lodgepole pine *(Pinus contorta)*
two needles per bundle
cones round, 1 to 2 inches long
red fir/lodgepole pine and subalpine forests

Pinyon pine *(Pinus monophylla)*
one needle per bundle
cones 1 to 2 inches long
dry, rocky slopes, mostly on eastern side of Sierra Nevada

True Firs: needles single, leaving a small round scar when falling from the twigs; cones always upright on branches; scales drop off, leaving central core of cone

Red fir *(Abies magnifica)*
needles somewhat four-sided
cones 4 to 8 inches long
mid-elevation forests

White fir *(Abies concolor)*
needles flat
cones 2 to 5 inches long
mixed conifer and red fir/lodgepole pine forests

Other Conifers:

Douglas fir *(Pseudotsuga menziesii)*
needles borne singly
cones with three-parted bract
mixed conifer forest

Giant sequoia *(Sequoiadendron giganteum)*
needles scalelike, thickly covering branches
cones 1 to 2 inches long
mixed conifer forest of central and
    southern Sierra Nevada

Mountain hemlock *(Tsuga mertensiana)*
needles single, arranged around the stem for
    bushy effect; leader at top of tree droops
cones 1 to 3 inches long
red fir/lodgepole pine and
    subalpine forests

Western juniper *(Juniperus occidentalis)*
needles scalelike
"cone" a purple, berrylike fruit
dry slopes and ridges, mostly on
    eastern side of Sierra Nevada

Incense cedar *(Calocedrus decurrens)*
needles scalelike, four-ranked, appearing
    whorled around stem
cones pendant, yellowish brown in color,
    about 1 inch long
reddish bark
middle and upper reaches of mixed
    conifer forest

Simple Key for Identifying Sierra Nevada Conifers

1. Leaves needlelike
    2. Needles borne in bundles or clusters, usually held together by thin sheath—*Pinus*
        3. Needles in clusters of five
            4. Cones slender
                5. Cones 10 to 20 inches long—*P. lambertiana*
                5. Cones 4 to 10 inches long—*P. monticola*
            4. Cones rounded in shape
                6. Cone scale with small incurved prickle—*P. balfouriana*
                6. Cone scale without prickle—*P. albicaulis*
        3. Needles in clusters of one to three
            7. Needles in clusters of three
                8. Cone scale turns outward—*P. ponderosa*
                8. Cone scale turns inward—*P. jeffreyi*
            7. Needles in clusters of one to two
                9. Needles in clusters of two—*P. contorta*
                9. Needles in clusters of one—*P. monophylla*

    2. Needles single
        10. Cones borne upright on the branch; needles leave a small, round scar when they fall—*Abies*
            11. Needles four-sided—*A. magnifica*
            11. Needles flat—*A. concolor*
        10. Cones not borne upright
            12. Cones with three-parted bract—*Pseudotsuga menziesii*
            12. Cones lacking three-parted bract—*Tsuga mertensiana*

1. Leaves scalelike, awl-shaped
    13. Cones 1 to 2 inches long, needles thickly covering branches—*Sequoiadendron giganteum*
    13. Cones otherwise
        14. "cone" a berrylike fruit—*Juniperus occidentalis*
        14. Cone pendant, flattened—*Calocedrus decurrens*

Terms You Should Know: An Illustrated Glossary

Botanical terminology has been simplified as much as possible in this book by describing plants in words familiar to most readers. However, for the sake of accuracy, exact botanical terms sometimes have been used. When you encounter such a term in the text, refer to the glossary for a definition and/or illustration.

PLANT PARTS

root. The root is the underground portion of the plant. Roots are of two main types: they may be fibrous, with many threadlike branches, or they may be taproots, consisting of a single, stout root and few branches. **Rootstocks** are underground stems that are rootlike and often produce additional stems at the joints.

stem. The stem grows upward from the root and has leaves, flowers, and fruits. Leaves are usually arranged in one of several ways along the stem:

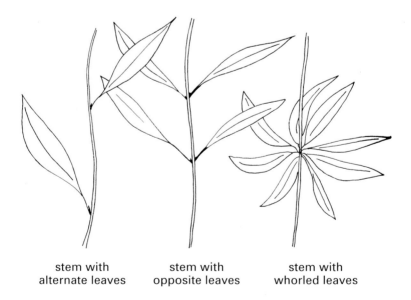

stem with
alternate leaves

stem with
opposite leaves

stem with
whorled leaves

leaves. Leaves are the part of a plant that produce sugar for plant growth. They may be simple or compound and come in a variety of shapes.

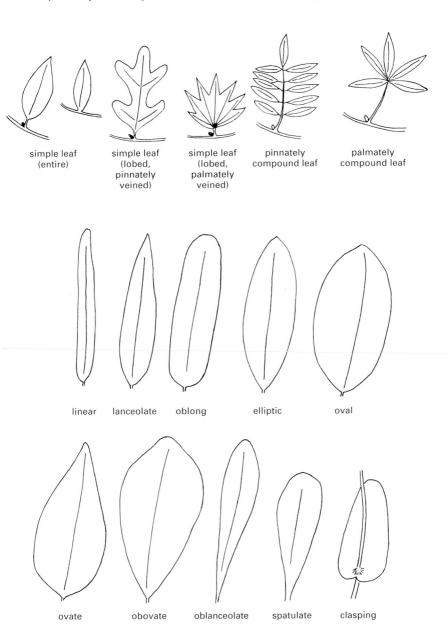

simple leaf (entire)

simple leaf (lobed, pinnately veined)

simple leaf (lobed, palmately veined)

pinnately compound leaf

palmately compound leaf

linear   lanceolate   oblong   elliptic   oval

ovate   obovate   oblanceolate   spatulate   clasping

flower. The flower is the part of the plant involved with reproduction. Flowers may be of several types, some containing only the female or seed-producing organs, some containing only the male or pollen-producing organs, others containing both. Some flowers lack the showy petals many associate with them.

Flowers consist of four basic parts: sepals, petals, stamens, and pistils.

Sepals are the outer circle of floral parts that protect the flower while it is developing. Often they resemble the petals, but are usually smaller and less conspicuous. Collectively, they are called the calyx.

Petals are the next circle of floral parts and are often brightly colored and conspicuous. This attracts bees, flies, and other pollinators. Sometimes they are joined together to form a basket or bell-shaped flower. Collectively they are called the corolla.

Stamens are arranged inside the petals and may be very numerous or of limited number. They contain the pollen.

Pistils are in the center of the flower and contain a platform to receive the pollen, either from the same plant or from another plant. Once fertilized, the flower develops into seeds that can grow into a new plant.

A typical flower is shown in the illustration below.

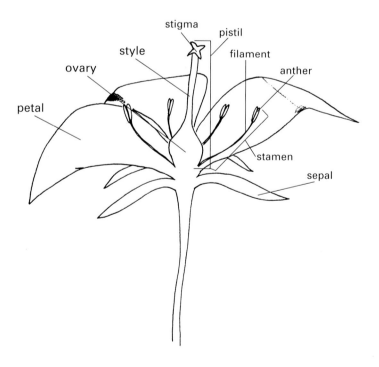

Glossary

alternate. Occurring singly, not opposite.

annual. Lasting only one year.

basal. At the base; for instance, leaves at the base of a plant.

bract. A small, modified leaf, usually at the base of a flower or cluster of flowers.

calyx. The outer circle of flower parts (sepals).

corolla. The inner circle of flower parts (petals).

cyme. A branched stalk of flowers where the central or uppermost flower opens before the flowers on the edge or bottom of the stalk.

decumbent. Lying down or growing along the ground.

desiccate. To dry up.

disk flower. The central, tubular flowers of a member of the sunflower family; for example, the yellow flowers in the center of a daisy.

elliptic. Oblong, with rounded ends.

endemic. A native plant growing only in a particular area.

habitat. The place where a plant grows.

head. A very close, compact cluster of flowers.

intergrade. To merge gradually, blending charateristics.

lanceolate. Lance-shaped, much longer than broad, but broader at the base and tapered at the tip.

leaflet. One of the parts of a compound leaf.

linear. Long, narrow, and with parallel sides.

oblanceolate. Lance-shaped, but broad at the tip and tapered at the base.

opposite. Occurring directly across from each other.

ovate. Shaped like an egg with the broadest part at the base.

panicle. Branched cluster of flowers where the lower flowers and those on the edge bloom before those at the bottom and inner part of the cluster.

parasite. Any organism obtaining nutrition by living in or on another organism.

pedicel. The stalk or stem of a single flower.

pendant. Hanging.

perennial. Lasting from one year to the next.

petal. One of the floral parts, usually colored.

petiole. The leaf stalk.

pistil. The central seed-bearing organ of a flower.

prostrate. Growing flat on the ground.

raceme. Unbranched cluster of pediceled flowers where the lower flowers open before those at the top.

ray flower. The flat, elongate flowers of a member of the sunflower family; for example, the white margin flowers of a daisy or the yellow flowers of a dandelion.

rootstock. An underground rootlike stem.

rosette. A collection of leaves arranged circularly around the base of a plant.

sepal. Parts of a flower just below the petals, usually green.

sessile. Stemless.

simple. One piece, as opposed to compound (in leaves).

spatulate. Narrow at the base and wide at the tip.

spike. Unbranched cluster of sessile flowers.

spur. Saclike or tubular projection from a sepal or petal.

stamen. The floral organ bearing the pollen.

subspecies. Geographically or morphologically isolated population of a larger-ranging species.

taproot. A stout, vertical root.

whorled. Three or more similar organs radiating from the same spot; for example, whorled leaves.

Selected References

Abrams, Leroy. [1940] 1960. *Illustrated Flora of the Pacific States.* 4 vols. Stanford, Calif.: Stanford University Press.

Ball, Edward K. 1972. *Early Uses of California Plants.* Berkeley, Calif.: University of California Press.

Forest Service, United States Department of Agriculture. 1937. *Range Plant Handbook.* Washington, D.C.: United States Government Printing Office.

Hall, Harvey M., and Carlotta C. Hall. 1912. *A Yosemite Flora.* San Francisco, Calif.: Paul Elder.

Hood, Bill, and Mary Hood. 1969. *Yosemite Wildflowers and Their Stories.* Yosemite, Calif.: Flying Spur Press.

Hickman, James C., ed. 1993. *The Jepson Manual: Higher Plants of California.* Berkeley, Calif.: University of California Press.

Johnston, Verna. 1994. *California Forests and Woodlands.* Berkeley, Calif.: University of California Press.

_____. 1970. *Sierra Nevada.* Boston, Mass.: Houghton Mifflin.

Muir, John. 1961. *The Mountains of California.* Garden City, N.Y.: The American Museum of Natural History, Doubleday and Company.

Munz, Phillip A., and David D. Keck. 1973. *A California Flora and Supplement.* Berkeley, Calif.: University of California Press.

Pool, Raymond J. 1941. *Flowers and Flowering Plants.* New York: McGraw-Hill.

Smiley, Frank J. 1921. *A Report upon the Boreal Flora of the Sierra Nevada of California.* Berkeley, Calif.: University of California Press.

Smith, Gladys L. 1973. *A Flora of the Tahoe Basin and Neighboring Areas.* San Francisco, Calif.: University of San Francisco.

Thompson, Steven, and Mary Thompson. 1972. *Wild Food Plants of the Sierra.* Berkeley, Calif.: Dragtooth Press.

Index

Elizabeth L. Horn —Malcolm Horn photo

About the Author

Elizabeth L. Horn holds a bachelor's degree in biology from Valparaiso University and a master's degree in plant ecology from Purdue University. Her interest in mountain wildflowers blossomed while she was a ranger-naturalist at Crater Lake National Park. She later embarked on a long career with the U.S. Forest Service and currently serves as director of public and governmental relations for the Forest Service's Northern Region. Ms. Horn has written several wildflower guides, including *Coastal Wildflowers of the Pacific Northwest*. She lives with her family in Missoula, Montana.

We encourage you to patronize your local bookstore. Most stores will order any title they do not stock. You may also order directly from Mountain Press, using the order form provided below or by calling our toll-free, 24-hour number and using your VISA, MasterCard, Discover or American Express.

Some other Natural History titles of interest:

____Beyond the Beach Blanket A Field Guide to Southern California Coastal Wildlife	$18.00
____Birds of the Northern Rockies	$12.00
____Birds of the Pacific Northwest Mountains	$14.00
____Botany in a Day	$22.50
____Coastal Wildflowers of the Pacific Northwest	$14.00
____Culinary Herbs for Short-Season Gardners	$20.00
____Desert Wildflowers of North America	$24.00
____Edible and Medicinal Plants of the West	$21.00
____From Earth to Herbalist An Earth-Conscious Guide to Medicinal Plants	$21.00
____An Introduction to Northern California Birds	$14.00
____An Introduction to Southern California Birds	$14.00
____Introduction to Southern California Butterflies	$22.00
____Mountain Plants of the Pacific Northwest	$25.00
____Northwest Weeds The Ugly and Beautiful Villains of Fields, Gardens, and Roadsides	$14.00
____Organic Gardening in Cold Climates	$12.00
____OWLS Whoo are they?	$12.00
____Plants of the Lewis & Clark Expedition	$20.00
____Plants of Waterton-Glacier National Parks and the Northern Rockies	$14.00
____Raptors of the Rockies	$16.00
____Roadside Plants of Southern California	$15.00
____Sagebrush Country A Wildflower Sanctuary	$14.00
____Sierra Nevada Wildflowers	$16.00
____Watchable Birds of the Great Basin	$16.00
____Watchable Birds of the Southwest	$14.00
____Wild Berries of the West	$16.00
____Wildflowers of Montana	$22.00
____Wyoming Wildflowers	$19.00

Please include $3.00 per order to cover shipping and handling.

Send the books marked above. I enclose $_____

Name_____

Address_____

City_____State_____Zip_____

☐ Payment enclosed (check or money order in U.S. funds)

Bill my: ☐VISA ☐ MasterCard ☐ Discover ☐ American Express

Card No._____Exp. Date:_____

Signature _____

MOUNTAIN PRESS PUBLISHING COMPANY

P.O. Box 2399 • Missoula, MT 59806
Order Toll Free 1-800-234-5308 • Have your credit card ready.
e-mail: info@mtnpress.com • website: www.mountain-press.com